Pulp

Editor: **Mike Evans**
Assistant Editor: **Humaira Husain**
Production Controller: **Candida Lane**
Picture Research: **Maria Gibbs**
Art Editor: **Valerie Hawthorn**
Design: **Ian Loats, Design Revolution**

Special thanks to Maria Jeffries, Melissa at Savage and Best

In memory of Johnny from S.I.N. who provided many
of the early Pulp photographs.

First published in 1996 by
Hamlyn, an imprint of
Reed Consumer Books Limited,
Michelin House, 81 Fulham Road,
London SW3 6RB
and Auckland, Melbourne, Singapore and Toronto

Copyright © 1996 Reed International Books Limited

A Catalogue record for this book is available from the British Library
ISBN 0-600-58974-9

Printed and bound in Great Britain by
Butler & Tanner Ltd, Frome and London

Pulp

PAUL LESTER

HAMLYN

CONTENTS

The Best Old Band In Britain 5

Happy Beginnings 9

The Legendary Years 21

London: Sex City 33

Razzmatazz 41

Welcome To The New Era 47

Masters Of The Universe 65

★★★★★★★★★★★★★★★★

The Best Old Band in Britain

Why Sheffield's Pulp have made it after seventeen years . . . their late Seventies and early Eighties peers . . . their contemporaries today . . . the group's fashion consciousness . . . their TV ubiquity . . . their love of musak and kitsch . . . high art or bad taste? . . . and are Pulp the northern Blur? . . .

IN the 1994/5 *Melody Maker* end of year readers' poll, Sheffield's finest, Pulp, scored an impressive number of votes for the section marked 'Best New Band In Britain'. Not bad considering they were about to enter their 18th year.

Pulp have a marvellous ability to, if not constantly reinvent themselves, then at least appear perennially fresh, 'with-it', up-to-date. Their astute musical and conceptual ideas, together with their absolute determination in the face of adversity and/or public disinterest, as well as a healthy dose of good fortune (their type of songs and methods have finally caught up with the times; either that or the zeitgeist has finally caught up with them) – all of this has led to Pulp looking and sounding, in 1996, like the most stylish contemporary pop group in the country.

When Pulp began, the groups who dominated music press discourse were the post-punk pioneers: PiL, Magazine, Joy Division and Wire, as well as fellow Sheffield synthpop innovators, Vice Versa (who soon became ABC), Human League (who later split into The League and Heaven 17), Cabaret Voltaire and Clock DVA.

Pulp have, subsequently, outlived such new sonic fads as white funk (Stimulin, Haircut 100), electro-pop (Depeche Mode, Soft Cell), new romantic (Duran Duran, Spandau Ballet), goth (Alien Sex Fiend, Sex Gang Children), 'C86' (The Bodines, Primal Scream), Madchester (Happy Mondays, The Stone Roses), shoegazing (Ride, Lush) and grunge (Nirvana, The Lemonheads) – not surprisingly, you can hear bits of some of these genres (as well as Seventies glam and disco) in the music of Pulp.

To put things into context, when Pulp formed, The Dooleys and Boney M were still popular. When Pulp played their first gig, Hot Chocolate were in the charts with 'No Doubt About It'. When Pulp recorded their first session for John Peel, New Order only had one LP in the shops. And Pulp's debut album came out three months before the debut single by a certain Manchester band called The Smiths, whose success was the cause of such grief on mainman Jarvis Cocker's part

Oasis, PiL, Blur and Human League – all are, or have been, peers of Pulp

in Pulp's miserable early days, because he considered they were covering fairly similar musical and lyrical terrain to Morrissey and Co.

Today, Pulp's peers are Britpop's big guns: Blur, Oasis, Elastica, Supergrass, Black Grape, Menswear and The Boo Radleys. Indeed, if Blur are The Beatles, Oasis are The Rolling Stones and Menswear are The Monkees of Britpop, then Pulp are The Velvet Underground – the colourful yet mysterious five-piece who exude alien strangeness, and who use striking avant-garde techniques and exotic/electric instrumentation (everything from violins to arcane Stylophones) to create something truly unique, something pop-not-pop, something arty *and* charty.

Pulp's novel approach to music-making may well recall the studio inventions of The Beatles, Can and Roxy Music, yet it's as now-sounding as Nineties pop experimentalists such as Pram and Stereolab. And lyrically, they evoke the incisive kitchen-sink mini-melodramas of Ray Davies and the vicious social commentary of Elvis Costello.

Pulp were once considered too weird to

be embraced by the mainstream, a right bunch of cults, all oblique melodies, obscure references, kitschadelic stage props (tin foil, anyone?) and jumble-sale chic goes space-age. These days, though, you can hardly switch on a radio or a TV without seeing Pulp performing one of their remarkable, and enormously infectious, fanfares for the common people.

Today, Pulp's unusual idea of what constitutes glamour (which Jarvis Cocker traces back to the purple woolly tights and Batman mask he wore as a kid) and their Oxfam gladrags are *de rigeur*: you've only got to spend five minutes in the centre of the known pop universe – Camden – to see that.

A further example of Pulp's 'nowness' is their sly debunking of light entertainment images, which might explain why they would look as at home on *The Des O'Connor Show* as they would on some enigmatic, underground, black & white art house movie. It could also explain why Jarvis Cocker currently crops up on all sorts of mainstream television shows, from *Top Of The Pops* – which he regularly hosts – to *Pop Quiz* to *The Big Breakfast*.

Then there's their assimilation of easy listening sounds and styles: as you can tell from their records, Pulp are deadly serious about their love for such maestros of muzak as Burt Bacharach and Henry Mancini, while their celebration of all things square, flared and polyester is mirrored by the success of currently trendy so-uncool-they're-hip London niteries like Cheese and Indigo.

Jarvis Cocker's sleazy tales of unrequited love and sexual frustration teeter on that fine line between high art and bad taste and would make sense in a nightmare seaside variety club *or* in front of a sophisticated college audience.

In many ways, Pulp are the South Yorkshire Blur, by turns affectionately and critically portraying Northern prole culture, just as Blur do southern working-class life.

Right now, Pulp are everywhere you look, although, for 15 years, they were nowhere, virtually invisible to all but the sharpest media-trained eye.

This, then, is their story – and what a long, strange trip it's been, full of multiple line-up changes, bizarre religious sects, near-fatal accidents, drugs, wheelchairs, freaks and separations.

What was that word again? Remarkable.

★★★★★☆☆★★★★★★★★

Happy Beginnings

Jarvis Cocker forms his own band,
Arabicus Pulp, in 1978 . . . Pulp's on-
going obsession with outer space . . .
Jarvis' childhood . . . Punk rock hits
Sheffield . . . the *lederhosen* period . . .
Cocker Senior's disappearing act . . . the
group's debut gig . . . the John Peel radio
session . . . some early press notices . . .
local heroes . . . then Pulp Mark I split . . .

DEEP FRIED IN INTAKE

PULP were originally called Arabicus Pulp, named after a coffee bean commodity during one particularly stimulating lesson at the height of punk in 1978, at Jarvis Cocker's school – Sheffield City Comprehensive – in deepest, darkest South Yorkshire.

Jarvis – today a fully-fledged alternative sex dandy and fashion guru with legions of male admirers and female devotees, but back then just a skinny, bespectacled kid of 14 or 15 in bad hand-me-downs – remembered how he arrived at such an unusual, and unwieldy, name.

'We were in Economics and somebody had the *Financial Times*,' he recalled, 'that's how it happened. It was a very unwieldy name, so it soon became Pulp. Everyone hated it. People thought you'd coughed – "pulp" – and it was frequently spelled wrong. We've been billed as Pope and The Pulps. It's fine now. I like the idea that it means ephemeral material that gets thrown away, like the cheap novels printed on crap paper. People collect those books now. Things that are meaningless and throwaway often survive to define a period.'

There were several meaningful things that came to define the first key period in Jarvis Cocker's life – his childhood. Born in the Sheffield suburb of Intake on September 19th, 1963 (he's a Virgo, astrology buffs),

Jarvis Branson Cocker's earliest memory is of his mother breast-feeding his sister, Saskia.

'I remember asking for some and my mum told me I was too old,' he recollected.'I felt really left out!'

On a more serious note, when Jarvis was five years old, he contracted meningitis, which gave him permanently impaired eyesight and accounts for the thick-lensed glasses he wears to this day.

'I've since realised that there was quite a big chance that I might've died,' he said, with disarming candour. 'They got all the class I was in at school to write letters – they didn't exactly say, "Sorry you won't be around much longer", but they wouldn't have gone to so much trouble if they didn't think I was on my way out.

'Everyone bought me all these great presents because they thought I was going to die,' he remembered, touchingly, 'but they had to burn them all when I left the hospital in case they were contaminated. The only things I was allowed to take home were a couple of cheap, plastic spacemen that could be sterilised in boiling water.'

The plastic spacemen may well have been the start of Jarvis Cocker's well-known obsession with outer space . . .

'I grew up with programmes like *Star Trek* and *Space 1999*,' he said, 'which is why I didn't bother learning to ride a "Chopper" or whatever – I thought that, by 1985, they would have established bases on Mars and everyone would be using hoverbikes.'

It was probably the milk-bottle spectacles that helped Jarvis develop: first, his feeling of being an outsider; second, his dry, drole sense of humour; and, third, his innate desire for revenge – by becoming a successful pop star – on those who cast aspersions on his early nerdish appearance.

'Actually, I don't know if it really was revenge,' corrected Jarvis, with the benefit of 20/20 hindsight. 'They say that success is partly revenge, your chance to get back at the people who took the piss out of you when you were young. But I'd have to be quite a sad person if I said I was still trying to prove the school bullies wrong 20 years on.'

Either way, Jarvis' hefty specs have, over the years, earned him numerous comparisons – some quite favourable, others downright insulting – ranging from Fifties rocker Buddy Holly to permanently be-shaded Sixties crooner Roy Orbison to silent movie star Harold Lloyd to comedian Eric Morecambe to eccentric playwright Alan Bennett to actor Michael Caine-circa-*The Ipcress File* (in fact, Jarvis recreated the latter's alternative secret agent look for *Select* magazine in 1994).

The clothes that his mum (a bit of a beatnik, apparently, all jeans and sandals and Miles Davis records, who bummed around Europe, started art college, then became pregnant with Jarvis, thereby ending her bohemian days, sacrificing a promising career as an artist to bring up her children and work as a fruit machine-emptier) dressed him in just made him feel even more different to his classmates.

'My uncle married a German woman, and their relatives used to send me leather shorts – *lederhosen* – the sort that Austrian goatherds wear, with a picture of a stag on the bib. Mum thought they were really cute,' he said, pausing for comic effect. 'I went to school looking like an extra from *Heidi*, or an Alpine shepherd boy. It was mortifying.

'Of course,' he carried on, in typically lugubrious manner, 'in a school in the suburbs of Sheffield, this wasn't normal behaviour. I managed to cajole my grandmother into buying me some normal shorts, and I'd change on the way to school. People would generally call me names and think I was odd.

'Around Sheffield, I was always getting flak off football fans – you know the kind of thing, "Fucking poof!" and stuff like that. I was always considered a bit effete. And at school, they thought I was a swot. I was lanky and I had braces on me teeth – I was pretty much a mess. I didn't get beaten up, though, because I could tell jokes. I always wanted to fit in.'

If the *lederhosen* weren't bad enough, there were also the skinny-rib jumpers that were so long they would hang over his shorts like a dress; his hair which his mum, in a bid to keep in touch with her hippychick roots, refused to cut ('I was the only boy at school who looked like a gawky girl'); and his yob-magnet name.

'That was a cross to bear,' he said, 'although now I think it's all right. I don't know why I was called Jarvis – my mum going to art college, probably, which may explain why my sister's called Saskia: she was Rembrandt's wife.'

The next key event occurred when Jarvis was seven: his father left home to go and live in Australia, where he lied and told everybody he was the brother of that other

Steve Mackey, bassman extraordinaire

famous Cocker from Sheffield, Sixties belter Joe (of 'With A Little Help From My Friends' and 'Up Where We Belong' fame), and landed a job as a rock DJ.

'He was a bit of a musician and a bit of an actor,' Jarvis has said of the 'Billy Liar' father who bequeathed to his son the ability to daydream one's fantasies into reality. 'He went to Australia to avoid paying me mum alimony and conned his way onto a Sydney radio station pretending to be Joe Cocker's brother. They believed him.'

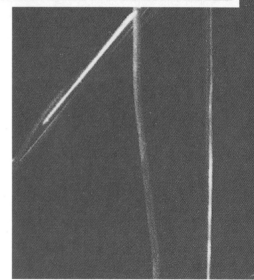

Jarvis Cocker, in his bohemian chic period

One day, this man will be a sex god

Jarvis hasn't seen his dad since, although he did speak to him about three years ago when Saskia got married and he rang up from Australia – it was Jarvis' first conversation with him for 21 years.

'I was stood there thinking, "This should be a really big moment in me life, this, I'm talking to me dad." You feel there should be this bond between you because you've come out his tail, but you're a stranger to him, you've got nothing in common.'

'It was very funny,' he said, unconvincingly. 'I mean, not funny at all. It was tragic, actually.'

More often than not, Jarvis is flippant when asked to reflect on his old man's disappearing act. As he told me in a lengthy interview in 1995 (from which many of the quotations and reminiscences in this book are taken): 'All the dads in our area seemed to leave around the same time, in 1970. Maybe they all got together and planned it.'

When he does reminisce about his father, he does so in a throwaway way: apparently, he used to sing in the bath; he could play the trombone; he was in a 12-piece jazz-rock band called Life On Mars; when he used to burp, he always said Archbishop Of Canterbury 'in a burpy voice'; and his 'scrotum was like a bag of marbles – it looked like there were about 10 in there.'

Jarvis has said that the only things he inherited from his dad were a taste for facial hair – coincidentally, he grew a beard at exactly the same age as did Cocker Senior – and a tendency to be rather maudlin, on occasion even depressive.

'I do get bad sometimes,' he admitted, 'but I try and supress that part of my personality because I realise that there's nothing good about it, that there's nothing to be gained from being depressed. So I usually just kind of pretend it isn't happening, and do something else.

'I mean,' he added, 'if you feel shit, instead of staying in and dwelling on it, you should just go out and try and take your mind off it, or try and get involved in something else, something manual – like mending the television or record player.'

One can't help but detect a note of sadness in the wry way Jarvis has dismissively treated the matter of his dadless youth, especially when he said, 'I think a lot of the reason I found it difficult when I started going out with girls was because I was brought up around so many of them.

'Through a biological accident,' he went on, 'there are lots more females than males in my family and I just thought of them as friends and considered myself to be the same as them. But when you start going out with people, you start to realise that that battle of the sexes thing does exist.'

Not that Jarvis has ever believed that he missed out in any way by his having only one natural parent.

'No way,' he frowned. 'That always gets me – the assumption that, if you've been brought up in a one-parent family, then that's it, you're the product of a broken home, yet another symptom of society's decay. I mean, my mother was very strict. If you wouldn't stand still when you were having your hair brushed, you got the hair brush broken over your head.

'You know those ones with the white plastic spines?' he asked in his deep, deadpan voice, gearing up for the laconic punchline to this tragicomic tale. 'I've had so many of them broken over my head. In the end, she started buying wooden brushes and things got really dangerous.'

Very funny, very sad. Very Pulp.

Even in the early days, Jarvis had an almost messianic hold over a crowd

Jarvis entertains the common people

MIS-SHAPES

WHEN punk came to Sheffield in the late Seventies, the young Jarvis Cocker was finally able to take advantage of his physical uniqueness and make it work for, rather than against, him, punk being all about the underdog, the outsider, the freak, the social misfit.

Jarvis chose the occasion of punk rock band The Stranglers playing a gig in Sheffield as his excuse for putting to the test his new-found confidence – between the ages of 14 and 17, Jarvis hardly left his bedroom, spending his time collecting *Planet Of The Apes*, *Bleep And Booster* and *Joe 90* annuals instead.

The Stranglers in action

The gig also provided Jarvis the opportunity to try out his brand new thrift-store jacket and the blue tie that his mother had crocheted for him. However, when Jarvis turned up at the concert alone – no one else he knew was interested in going – he soon discovered that, even in his full New Wave regalia, he was still not going to be allowed to Join In.

'All these people in mohicans took the piss out of me and called me a mod,' he said, somewhat poignantly.

Undeterred, Jarvis – who had 'always wanted to be in a pop group' (note his choice of words: 'pop', not 'rock'; 'group', not 'band') because it was the only opportunity, as he saw it, for a weirdo like him to actually fit in – finally decided to form an actual group at school, after years of wandering from the classroom to the dinner queue to the playground convinced that he already was a pop star.

'I don't know what a pop star personality is,' he said, 'but I wanted to be in a group from a really early age and used to pretend that I was. When I was about 12 or 13, at school, there was a gang of about five of us and we were all in a group. I'd say, I'm the singer, he's the drummer, and stuff like that. It just made it seem more interesting when you were walking down the corridor, imagining that we were all in a group with all the other kids clapping us.'

Some time in 1978, the dream became reality (sort of, anyway) when Jarvis and a few mates started practising in his mother's living room on Friday nights after school, inspired by the punk rock philosophy that 'anyone can do it' (which was quite handy since, as Jarvis recalls, 'none of us had any ability at that point'). They acquired a £10 drum kit from his mum's boyfriend's dad, who knew people in an old dance band, and his mum put the group's name – first Arabicus Pulp, then just plain Pulp – on the front of the kit using Sellotape.

As Jarvis recounted in a recent issue of *Record Collector* magazine, the first thing Pulp were able to present to the public was a Super 8 film in 1979 (when Cocker was a fifth former). The main attraction of the film was a bizarre silent extravaganza called *Spaghetti Western Meets Star Trek* in which Pulp's head honcho played Clint Eastwood beamed down onto a planet where all the inhabitants were extras from *The Good, The Bad, And The Ugly.*

This was also the first time Pulp actually made a profit, having charged everyone 10p to watch the mini-spectacular during lunchtime – 'we made about 10 quid.'

Pulp had just entered the music business.

Jarvis and Steve in moody mood

Candida, Russell and Jarv *au naturel*

LOOKING FOR LIFE

JARVIS Cocker is the only surviving member of Pulp Mk 1. Since those early days, approximately one and a half dozen Pulp musicians have come and gone, some of them disappearing without trace, others having found rather more interesting ways to pass the time – like drugs. Or religion.

'There was a time when it seemed as though everyone who had ever been in the band had left to join the charismatic Christians,' said Jarvis.

Today's line-up of Russell Senior (guitar, violin), Steve Mackey (bass), Candida Doyle (organ, synthesiser, Stylophone) and Nick Banks (drums) solidified between the early and late Eighties, Russell joining first in 1984

and Steve being the last new recruit, having teamed up with Jarvis after meeting him at art college in London in 1988.

The very first incarnation of Pulp, however, comprised Peter Dalton on guitar, Mark Swift on drums and David 'Fungus' Lockwood on bass, although by the time the group made their debut appearance at the Rotherham Arts Centre in July 1980 (to which they turned up in a mobile grocer's van), old Fungus had been replaced by Philip Thompson because the former played too fast, so keen was he to get to the end so he could go and eat. Pulp were rapturously described at the time as 'like a cross between Abba and The Fall.'

Having got Rotherham to surrender to

Pulp's charms, it was now Sheffield's turn to succumb. And so, the following month, Pulp played at the celebrated Leadmill club, second from the bottom of the bill of an all-dayer, performing covers of 'Stepping Stone', 'Wild Thing', 'House Of The Rising Sun' and Motorhead's version of Holland-Dozier-Holland's 'Leaving Here'.

It was a disaster: they'd got in a new drummer, Jimmy Sellers, who was more interested in drinking than playing, and the bassist, who didn't understand the finer points of amps and PAs and such, got drowned in a sea of feedback, panicked and proceeded to fall off the stage, the cause of much hilarity in the crowd.

Things could only get better.

One of Pulp's early incarnations. Yes, that *is* Jarvis with an eyepatch

COUNTDOWN

DUE to his interest in the synth-based pop of local boys The Human League and Cabaret Voltaire, as well as keyboards-based Sixties outfits like The Doors and The Velvet Underground, Jarvis bought a Moog synthesizer and a Casio Tone, getting Peter Dalton to play them instead of his guitar (Jarvis took over six-string chores himself) replacing Philip Thompson with Jamie Pinchbeck on bass, and drafting in Wayne Furniss to play drums.

This was the line-up responsible for many crucial Pulp firsts: their first demo tape in early 1981; their first session for John Peel in November 1981, the result of much plucking up of courage on Cocker's part

Steve and Jarv at (John) Peel Acres

when Peel did a road show at Sheffield Polytechnic, Jarvis thrusting the tape in the DJ's hand, never expecting to hear from him again; their first music press interview with *Melody Maker* in January 1982; and their very first release in June 1982 – a track entitled 'What Do You Say?' for a compilation called 'Your Secret's Safe With Us'.

In a recent interview with *Melody Maker*, John Peel expressed his admiration for the session ('For people unfamiliar with a big studio and not having done many gigs at that time, it sounds pretty good,' he said), although Jarvis himself winces when he thinks about these early recordings.

The session was recorded with, among other amateurish things, a drum made up of an old electronic calculator and one of those pressure-sensitive mats normally used for burglar alarms, much to the shock and horror of the producer, Dale Griffin ('I think he was disgusted,' said Jarvis).

Of the four tracks, 'Refuse To Be Blind' is a Gary Numanoid, sci-fi drone complete with unnerving Dalek voices; 'Turkey Mambo Momma' sounds like a cross between Magazine, turn-of-the-decade avant-dance Mancunians, A Certain Ratio, and those android New Wavers from Akron Ohio, Devo; 'Wishful Thinking' is a gentle ballad that would crop up later on Pulp's debut album, 'It'; and 'Please Don't Worry' is a neat slice of electro-pop which includes the amusing line, 'Just think of all the money that's gone to your waist.'

Melody Maker's Frank Worrell described the session at the time as 'deliciously innocent pop', going on to extol the twin virtues of Jarvis Cocker In Person ('the tallest teenager I've ever shook hands with, all splashes of wild colour, off-beat clothes and hair and an underlying purity that doesn't seem to fit') and Pulp Live.

'Pulp live are a carnival of lunacy,' wrote Worrell of Pulp's performance art, 'probably the future focus of live performance in essence: humour, participation, letting your hair down, but backed by a whirling synthesizer pop which ultimately keeps the party punching.'

A review from the now-defunct pop weekly, *Sounds*, was slightly less ecstatic – 'Pulp are the musical equivalent of a Milky Way bar, a band you can listen to without ruining your appetite for something more substantial' – although the Sheffield-based fanzine, *Pink Rag*, more than made up for it, describing Pulp as 'unpredictable, wacky, yet possibly brilliant outsiders.'

Not surprisingly, the young Jarvis Cocker believed this frenetic burst of Pulp activity, together with all the excitable reactions, to be the preamble to some kind of dizzy overnight success.

'I thought I was going to be a child star,' he has said. 'I was still at school when John Peel's producer rang up my mother. We got onto the front page of the *Sheffield Star* – we became the stars of the school for a bit. The paper actually wanted to take pictures of us in our school uniform and pictures of us in our stage gear – a sort of before and after thing – and we refused to do 'em. We were awkward even then.

'But It was a really magical time. I remember thinking that this was it, that it was music all the way for me from then on. So I decided I wasn't going to go to university (he had a place at Liverpool University to read English Literature). I was going to stay in Sheffield and carry on with the group.'

So certain was Jarvis that God was smiling down upon him that he auditioned for a job as presenter on Channel 4's anarchic new 'yoof' television show, *The Tube*. Although unsuccessful, the fact that Jarvis actually went for it speaks volumes about his increasing self-assurance as he approached his twenties.

Unfortunately, the rest of the group weren't quite so convinced that stardom was just a synth doodle away, and in July 1982, Pulp fell apart – unlike Jarvis, Jamie and Peter did want to go to university.

Besides, Peter's dad, a headmaster, threatened to pour his dinner over his potentially wayward son's head if he refused to quit the group.

Pulp in their arty, experimental, weird middle period

★★★★★★★★★★★★★★★★★★

The Legendary Years

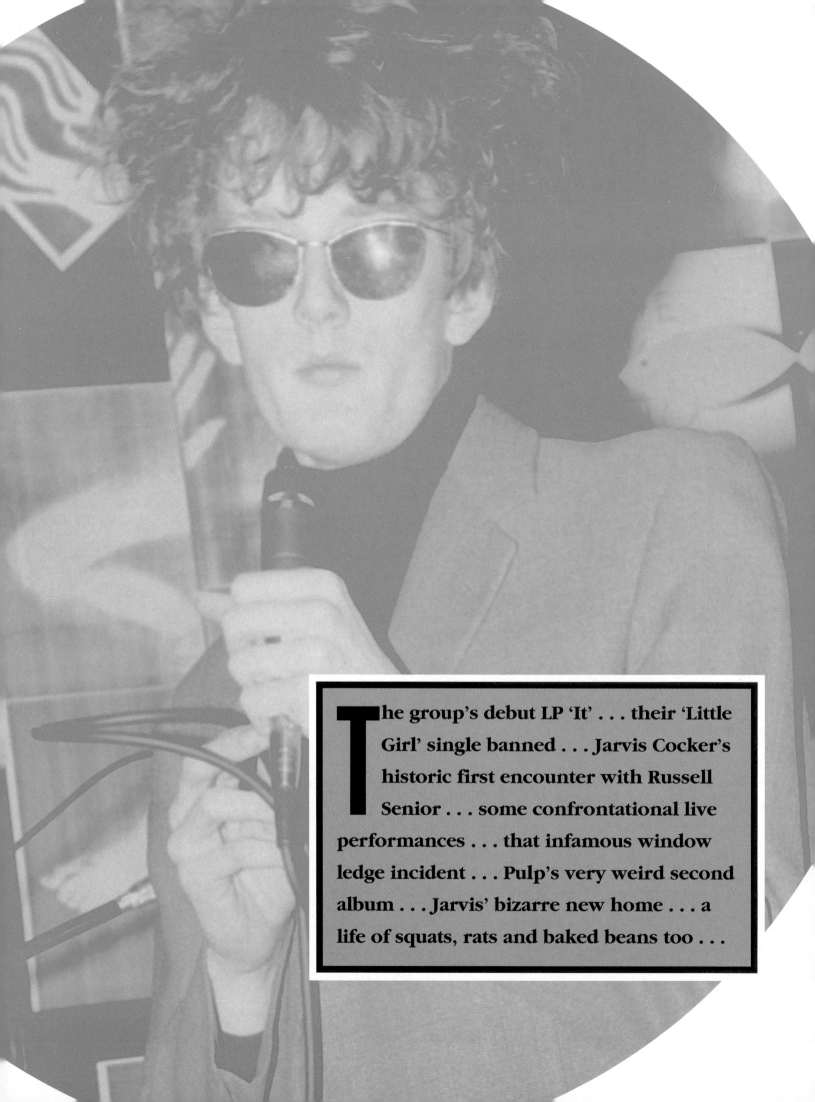

The group's debut LP 'It' . . . their 'Little Girl' single banned . . . Jarvis Cocker's historic first encounter with Russell Senior . . . some confrontational live performances . . . that infamous window ledge incident . . . Pulp's very weird second album . . . Jarvis' bizarre new home . . . a life of squats, rats and baked beans too . . .

THAT'S 'IT'!

SO Jarvis had to start from scratch.

Almost, anyway. Wayne Furniss was still around, but he was just one of many new recruits – including Saskia Cocker and Jarvis' old school flame Gill Taylor on vocals, Mister Barry Thompson, formerly of the Syd Lawrence Orchestra, on drums, and Simon Hinkler, future member of goth rockers The Mission, on keyboards – who all featured on what was to become Pulp's debut LP, 'It'.

The title came about because 'Pulp' plus 'It' made 'Pulpet'.

'It was all about the idea of preaching to people,' said Jarvis.

The music itself was inspired by Leonard Cohen ('We were definitely anti-rock at the time') and was recorded in a hideous, broken-down studio in Sheffield with just one microphone. The album was released by York label Red Rhino, in March 1983.

Track one, side one – 'My Lighthouse' – was generally considered to be the best of a bad bunch, and came out as a single the following month. Jarvis himself is rather dismissive about this tentative first collection of songs about girls and boats and trains.

'You can just hear the naivety on it,' he cringed recently. 'It embarrasses me. I was writing all these really direct love songs about girls and I'd never had a proper girlfriend. Mind you, I had just left school.'

'It' is actually rather better than Jarvis remembers: it's a selection of wistful, mainly acoustic ballads full of self-doubt, premature disillusionment, yearning and Jarvis' rich, dark Scott Walker/Julian Cope-ish croon. 'Wishful Thinking', 'In Many Ways' and, in particular, the plaintive, hauntingly lovely 'Blue Girls', are certainly worthy additions to the Pulp oeuvre, delightful snapshots of a group in their infancy.

'The most suprising thing about "It" is how ambitious it sounds today,' wrote *Select*

on the LP's re-release in March 1995, 'all big production, "Astral Weeks"-like flutes and breathy female backing vocals. Whereas Pulp in '95 are all about sex, oddball glamour and brilliantly-detailed story-telling, the 1983 model were angsty and lovelorn contemporaries of Felt and The Smiths. "It" is an interesting relic of distant times.'

LIFE MUST BE SO WONDERFUL

'IT' actually got a few good reviews on its release as well, but nobody bought it, which is perhaps why Pulp's then-manager, Tony Perrin, suggested to Jarvis that he should take the group in a more commercial, Wham!-inspired direction – George Michael, Andrew Ridgeley, their shuttlecocks and their 'Club Tropicana' were absolutely massive at the time.

Hence, the brass-laden debacle that was 'Everybody's Problem', the single that was released in September 1983 (their last for

Pulp in their natural habitat – Sheffield

'Help! I can't get this chip out of my mouth!'

Red Rhino) and which bombed so spectacularly that poor Jarvis almost gave up there and then.

Jarvis spent the next few months signing on ('Everybody did it. It was the golden age of dole culture') and generally wandering round Sheffield wondering how and when to give Pulp their one last shot at the big time.

Then, in the middle of 1984, Pulp changed shape again, thanks to a chance encounter with Russell Senior, who Jarvis had already met on two previous occasions.

The first time Russell bumped into Jarvis was after that debut Pulp gig at The Leadmill in 1980, which Senior reviewed for his fanzine, *The Bath Banker*.

The next time they met was at the fishmarket where Jarvis' mum had made him get a job because she thought it would be a chance for him to make friends and be a bit more 'normal'. He'd had other odd-jobs – plagroup leader, bingo caller at kids parties – but as a fishmonger Jarvis really excelled.

'He'd charm all these old ladies into buying more crabs than they needed,' Russell told *The Face*. 'They loved him.'

Sadly, the girls around Sheffield weren't so keen on the boy who reeked of haddock and bleach – Jarvis would turn up at parties after a hard Saturday's work, smelling both of fish and the disinfectant he used to try and remove the pong.

Anyway, Jarvis, Russell, new drummer Magnus Doyle, new bassist Pete Mansell and keyboardist Tim Allcard (also responsible for poetry recitations and weird factory siren noises) formed the latest incarnation of Pulp.

Not that it lasted long, mind: their first gig, in front of a rugby crowd at Brunel University in September 1984, ended in a bottle-smashing and fist-flying riot after Allcard's esoteric ruminations on the nature of existence got a bit too fanciful and abstract for the beer boys in the crowd.

'We were quite confrontational back then,' said Jarvis, as ever the master of the understatement.

Russell's Dada-esque, surrealist play, *The Fruits Of Passion*, which Pulp performed on several occasions as support to other

The grim days of the mid-Eighties

never had to wonder / Which one he's going to fill'), which earned Pulp a radio ban.

Jarvis maintains to this day that the song was never designed to shock – in fact, he insists he wrote it after he saw a photograph of his mum on her wedding day and realised how young she was to give up all her hopes and dreams for the twin responsibilities of marriage and children.

There were greater calamities to come than radio bans, however. Three days before the release of 'Little Girl', in December 1985, the hapless Jarvis, in a foolish attempt to impress a girl by teetering around the outside edge of a tall building, slipped from the window ledge and fell more than 30 feet to the ground, causing injuries to his pelvis (which was fractured), wrist and ankle (which were smashed), putting him in hospital for six weeks and confining him to a wheelchair for two months.

Doctors said Jarvis would never walk properly again.

'It did me good, though,' he told *Vox*'s Max Bell in 1995, speaking of the accident which occurred as he sunk to an all-time spiritual low.

'It literally brought me down to earth,' he continued, 'beat all the aestheticism out of me. Before then, I thought I was sorted out to be a pop star. I had this very romanticised

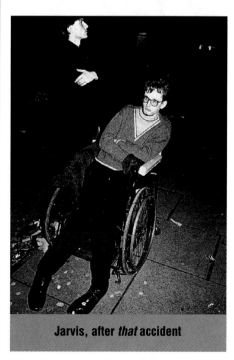

Jarvis, after *that* accident

groups, was unarguably the most confrontational, extreme thing they ever did, causing highly aggressive reactions around Britain towards the end of 1984, probably because, for its climactic scene, Jarvis had to (pretend to) consume a plate of dog faeces.

It didn't come as much of a suprise, then, when poor Tim Allcard decided to leave the group. He was soon replaced on keyboards by Magnus' sister, Candida.

Pulp as we know and adore them today were now three-fifths in place.

Not that it was plain sailing all the way from there into the Top 20 . . .

ACCIDENTS WILL HAPPEN

IN 1985, Pulp switched from Red Rhino to Fire Records, who gave the group enough money to record 'Little Girl (With Blue Eyes)', their third single.

Sung by Jarvis in booming, post-modern Englebert Humperdinck style, the song sounded pleasant enough (with its' shades of 'I'm Your Puppet', the Sixties soft-soul hit for James and Bobby Purify), but the lyric contained a seedy, near-pornographic account of a female of no fixed age ('*Little girl with blue eyes / There's a hole in your heart / And one between your legs / You've*

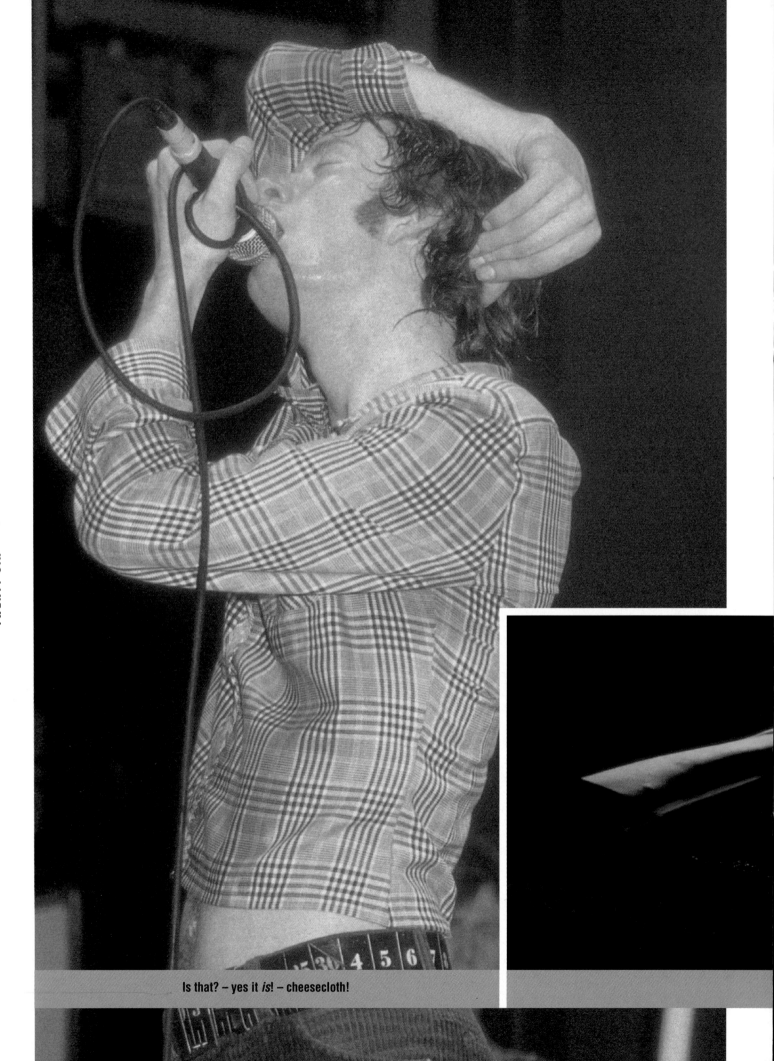

Is that? – yes it *is*! – cheesecloth!

view of life. I used to get up in the afternoon and avoid the obstacles of the mundane everyday. I'd done nothing except live in the future. But this was when my countdown period began. I was stuck in a ward with a lot of old blokes who'd worked down the pit, and talking to them made me alter my whole viewpoint. There's nothing quite like spending six weeks just lying flat on your back to help you take stock.'

But in a conversation with *Select* in 1994, Jarvis denied being so depressed that he actually climbed onto that window ledge because he wanted to put an end to his miserable existence.

'I was in poor spirits, but I wasn't trying to kill myself. I was just arseing around. But the first thing I thought was that I could have died and that it wouldn't have been noble or dramatic, it would have just been pathetic – me hanging there by my fingers saying "I can't get back in". At least in a film, there would have been drums or exciting string music or something.

'Falling out of that window made me realise there was no magical thread running through life. It's all random. But once you realise that, it's quite good.'

'FREAKS' SCENES

ANYONE remotely familiar with Pulp in 1995, in particular with Jarvis Cocker's sexily dexterous, limb-contorting stage movements, will realise that he defied medical expectations after all, to become a fully-functioning love god from the Planet Libido.

However, back in 1986, Jarvis hadn't yet realised just how good life could be. Because for Pulp, all that year could offer were yet more setbacks and missed chances.

It wasn't all doom and gloom. First, all the spare time that Jarvis had at his disposal gave him ample opportunity to develop his interest in jumble sale clothes and kitsch historical paraphernalia, enabling him to build up quite a collection of synthetic fashionwear (brown corduroy flared suits, dayglo crimplene shirts and such) and assorted Sixties/Seventies bric-a-brac – the kind of stuff for which Pulp, the doyens of Interstellar Thrift Store eccentricity, are now rightfully renowned.

At one point, the interest almost became an obsession.

'Maybe it was some kind of way of getting myself security, or something,' he said. 'I would never really bother taking the stuff out of the bags – just buying it was the thing. After a while, I could hardly get into my room.'

Jarvis also had enough free time to design the sleeve for the group's next release, the 'Dogs Are Everywhere' EP. The EP got its title after one particularly harrowing night which the comparatively puritanical Jarvis and Russell spent observing, from a safe distance, their rather less abstemious bandmates, Magnus and Peter, get pissed and stoned with a bunch of pals and behave in a thoroughly base fashion more befitting canines than humans. Then, 'Dogs' was made Single Of The Week by *Melody Maker* in June '86, the first time Pulp had received such an accolade.

On an equally 'up' note, the five-track EP contained some of Pulp's finest music and lyrics to date: the deceptively gentle title cut, the robotic disco-influenced 'Mark Of The Devil', the rumbling, bass note-led 'Aborigine', the funereal ballad 'Goodnight' and '97 Lovers', the latter featuring a story – all about his aunty having sex with his uncle in her bedroom underneath a poster of Roger Moore, apparently – of which Jarvis was rather proud.

These five tracks, as well as the three

Jarvis Cocker: King of the Jumble (Sale)

The two faces of Jarvis

songs from the 'Little Girl' single, the pair from Pulp's January '87 release, 'They Suffocate At Night', and the couple from March '87's 'Master Of The Universe' single, all appear on the Fire compilation, 'Masters Of The Universe', which was eventually released in June 1994.

But even the world's greatest optimist could see that, for Pulp at this stage in their career, the cons outweighed the pros by roughly ten-to-one.

For their live shows, Jarvis had to sing and perform from a wheelchair (this is perhaps where he learned to use his hands in the expressive, threatrical manner to which we have now become accustomed). Some actually believed this to be some kind of disability chic gimmick, along the lines of Morrissey and his infamous hearing aid, a crass attempt to physically demonstrate emotional crippledom.

The gigs themselves were a travesty, Magnus having to continually reassemble his drum kit after trashing it between songs; their fans, reckons Jarvis, 'all seemed to be mentally unbalanced'; The Smiths were entering their most successful phase while Pulp, obviously, were not; and Jarvis was in the middle of his first long-term relationship, one of those horribly debilitating affairs that usually drag on for about 18 months past their sell-by date.

'Somehow,' wrote an *NME* reviewer covering one of Pulp's gigs around this time, 'it's nice to think that there is a far corner of Sheffield that will forever be experimental and out on a limb. Even if it's not very good. Because it's not very good.'

'Those were dark days,' the singer almost shuddered at the memory of this grim period, 'the low-point, emotionally, of my life.'

'THE HORROR, THE HORROR'

AND then, all of a sudden, Pulp recorded their second LP in one week and at a cost of £600.

The album's sleeve photography featured various grotesquely distorted images of the group and bore the sub-title, 'Ten Songs About Power, Claustrophobia, Suffocation And Holding Hands'.

The music was equally bleak and unsettling. 'Fairground', with its eerie fairground organ and stop-start, quiet-harsh structure, was quite unpleasant. 'I Want You' was a Velvets-circa-'Pale Blue Eyes' menacing ballad. 'Being Followed Home' and 'They Suffocate At Night' heightened the all-pervading atmosphere of anxiety, paranoia, fear and suspicion, while 'The Never-Ending Story' and 'Don't You Know' addressed such funtime popsong themes as pain, repulsion, nausea and revenge.

Then there was 'Master Of The Universe', just another everyday neo-Nietschean account of domination, masturbation and submission, and 'Life Must Be So Wonderful', which was downright disturbed (*'You rot in your bedroom / You cry on the phone / I'm sorry but he's not home . . . I smile whilst you fall apart'*). 'There's No Emotion' said it all.

The Joy Division-like 'Anorexic Beauty' (dedicated to Lena Zavaroni, celebrated child star and victim of a severe eating disorder for years), journeyed further still into the heart of darkness, a graphic morality tale (*'Anorexic beauty, underweight goddess/Sitting alone on a cold bar stool . . . pastel white features/scarlet-bloodied lips and deathly tones/The girl of my nightmares/sultry and corpse-like'*) which showed once and for all exactly whose side Pulp were on, that of life's misfits, mistakes and mis-shapes.

Pulp's second album could quite easily have been titled 'Ghouls', 'Horrorshow' or 'Alien Nation'. It was called 'Freaks'.

'It was called "Freaks" because I was worried that I was turning into a freak,' said Jarvis, the eternal neurotic boy outsider, and as blunt as ever. 'I'd been out of school for four years, living this marginal life with no success. Then I moved into this old steel factory above a street theatre company in the centre of town – my friend was the caretaker, so I lived there rent-free – and things really became weird.

'Part of it had been turned into rehearsal rooms,' he explained 'and there was a model railway enthusiast upstairs, along with two

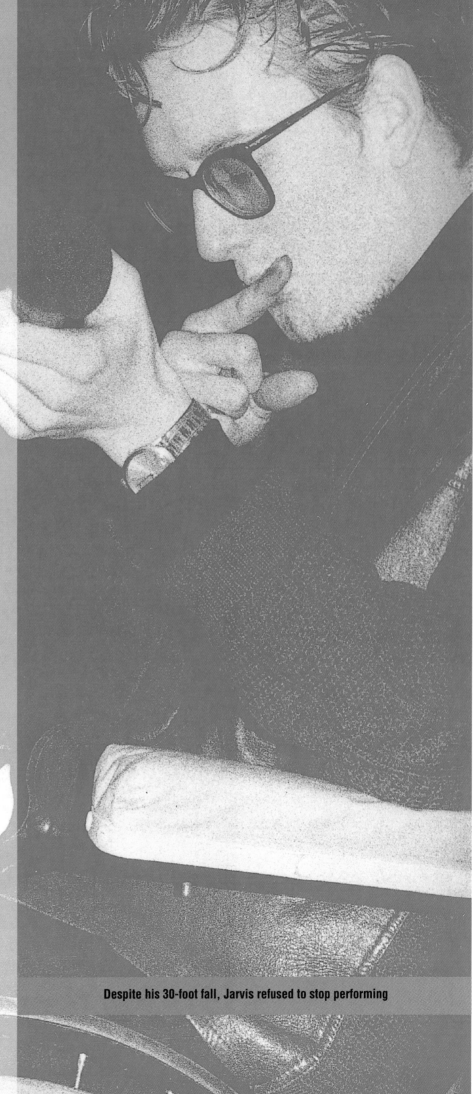

Despite his 30-foot fall, Jarvis refused to stop performing

table-tennis clubs. There was a feud going on between them – they used to shit in front of each other's doors. Pretty soon, the place became a magnet for all the freaks, misfits and drop-outs of Sheffield.

'There were all these travelling, crusty, vegan, circus types everywhere as well,' he carried on down memory lane, 'with names like Tarquin, and they were all into stone circles and smoking joints and stuff. They were all minted and it was all, "Yeah, man" and "absolutely terrible, yah" and they all seemed to be jugglers.

'Trouble was, they decided to start up this whole food cooperative thing – "Yeah, man, we'll cut out the middle man" – which eventually brought loads of rats into the building. Rats were shitting in all the muesli and pulses, but they still kept flogging it to people! You know: "Get some free rat shit with your mung beans!" or whatever.'

Indeed, when *Melody Maker*'s Paul Mathur ventured northwards to Steel City in the summer of 1986 to visit Jarvis and Co in squatland for the group's second major interview – whose purpose was to promote 'Dogs Are Everywhere' – he found himself having to negotiate a treacherous path between the ceiling-high mounds of Heinz Baked Beans tins which filled up Pulp's delightful abode.

Were they, wondered the journalist, the result of some kind of profound philosophical/artistic insight from the warped minds of this bizarre northern pop group re: 20th Century life and culture? Apparently not. One of the squatters just happened to really like baked beans.

'My life had no shape and no discipline during this period, basically. All in all, I was not a happy person,' summed up Jarvis. 'Things with the band weren't great, either. Magnus and Pete would smoke dope all day and have endless arguments with Russell, who at that time was in his very strict disciplinarian phase.

'We had been doing something both worthwhile and original, but no one seemed to be interested.'

Not yet, anyway.

'Mother, is that you?'

★★★★★☆★☆☆★☆★★★★★

London: Sex City

The umpteenth incarnation of Pulp dissolves . . . Jarvis makes the momentous decision to move to London . . . celibacy and film school . . . the Ecstasy Generation's impact on Jarvis . . . more record company hassles halt Pulp's progress

Set The World On Fire

'Oh, woe is me!'

FON FON FON

ON the video set for the 'They Suffocate At Night' single, some time in early 1987, Pulp split up, Jarvis deciding 'it wasn't worth the aggro anymore.'

Out went Pete and Magnus, and then, after a period where players seemed to join and leave on an hourly basis (one bassist, Stephen Havenhand, had to go because he was too shy, while another, Anthony Genn, flipped out after a bad experience with acid – he later became a born-again Christian), Nick Banks became Pulp's drummer.

Next problem: Jarvis realised he'd used up all his songs. So, pissed off with Fire for, among other things, failing to transform Pulp into global megastar household names, he started getting involved with Sheffield's Fon label, recording a series of new tracks influenced by the then-burgeoning House and Acid scenes.

'Don't You Want Me Anymore' (which was subsequently re-recorded for the 'Separations' LP), 'Rattlesnakes' (which never eventually came out) and 'Death Comes To Town' (later retitled 'Death II') were, considered Jarvis, 'our best recordings ever, done in a proper studio with as much time as we needed and a string section.'

But?

'But Fon decided not to release them.'

CAPITAL GAINS

'THE sky is crying out tonight/The need to leave this town' – 'Countdown', from 'Separations'.

There was only one thing for it – to get out of Sheffield.

'I'd spent the best part of a decade in an unsuccessful group,' said Jarvis. 'I was forced to admit I'd been wasting my time. It's humiliating. But it was doing my head in. If I didn't get out of Sheffield sharpish, I knew I was going to end up as a sad character who used to be in a band.'

So, in 1988, Jarvis moved to The Smoke, where he managed to get a place studying film-making at Central London's highly respected St Martin's College Of Art.

'I'd heard about St Martin's, read about it

in books, and thought, This is going to be the glamour I've been looking for, there in the capital city it will occur.'

Naurally, this being the history of Jarvis Cocker – described variously as 'the kid from *Kes* 20 years on', as 'Woody Allen in platform heels', and as 'Jilted John Travolta' – there was no social whirl, at least not in his part of town. Furthermore, the culture shock was considerable, as he explained to Andrew Smith of *The Face*.

'In my naivety, I thought the whole world was like Sheffield. When I found myself in a different environment, I thought, "I'd better write all this stuff down before I forget it, because I'm not living like that any more. People in London don't go round saying, "Ah, that's ace, that" or, "I fingered her at t'busstop – awright?"'

Pulp, as they might look in the year 2016

While Jarvis expected his move from the provinces to the capital to be the start of all manner of wonderful depravity and hedonistic activity, it actually spelled anonymity, isolation and, ultimately, celibacy for the man who remained a virgin until he was 19, the man they are now calling the sexiest pop star in Britain.

Jarvis Cocker abstained from sex for nearly four years.

'Makes you appreciate it when you finally get round to doing it!' he joked, going on to

'God, I'm gorgeous!'

Piccadilly palaver

explain to me why he considered sex to be an important lyrical subject: 'I don't think sex is the be-all and end-all of life. But I write about it quite a lot because I think it motivates people's actions a lot of the time.'

'Usually, sex is written about really badly in pop, mostly falling into that kind of parody of a man trying to portray himself as God's gift to women, being the greatest sex stud alive. It's not unusual to write about sex if you're a swingbeat or a rap artist, but it's certainly unusual if you're a white, northern bloke. Which is good, because no one like me is doing it right now – I saw a gap in the market, and I'm filling it!

'I wanted to write about sex in a less stupid and nebulous, more realistic, matter-of-fact way, in the context of other things like going to the shops or wondering whether you've got clean pants for tomorrow.

'Not that I espouse a free-and-easy attitude towards sex. In fact, television programmes like *The Good Sex Guide* can put you off sex forever – they're enough to make you celibate. They're like sex manuals.' He continued on this theme, adopting a posh BBC voice to make the point: '"Insert object A into slot B for 34 minutes and one should achieve orgasm."'

'Not enough is written about the psychological dimensions of it, though,' digressed Jarvis, widely regarded as the most forthright and astute sexpop wordsmith of the age. 'Sex is a very emotional thing. You have to be very close to the person you're doing it with. The intimacy is what turns me on.

'Mind you, that's what was hard for me at first, being quite reserved, being an inch away from someone, totally in someone else's personal space. You're literally on top of somebody – there's no escape.'

The 25-year-old Jarvis did, however, encounter some distractions in London . . .

'I thought I'd be mixing with the beautiful people of the film world, but it wasn't like that,' he said, honestly. 'But it was a good laugh. I was amazed when I first came to London: it was 1988 and Acid House was just starting to happen. I thought I was far too old to get into youth cults, but I just got swept away by it. So . . .'

So?

'So naturally I became a drug addict.'

He was being tongue-in-cheek, of course, and, in the wake of the 'Sorted For E's And Wizz' fiasco, we know where Jarvis really stands on the subject of drugs (see chapter seven). But he has had his moments, experimenting over the years with magic mushrooms ('I never really liked them. They destroyed your ego, made you analyse yourself too much'), dope ('It makes me feel panicky, like there's something wrong with my brain, like I'm doing it irreparable damage') and Ecstasy ('I liked that because it helped me feel less reserved').

It didn't take long before Jarvis started seeing through the E'd-up, smiley culture, Second Summer Of Love, goodwill-to-all-mankind vibe of the rave scene.

'Everybody kept coming up to you, saying, "All right, geezer!" and "sorted, sorted", "sweet!" – that sort of thing. But it never got any further than that. Because, at the end of the night, you'd walk out of the club or wherever, and people would just blank you and go back to being normal. I couldn't believe it at the time, the way they

'Any jokes about fags and you're dead!'

were all One Love one minute, and the next they just switched off.

'The thing about rave was, you might go out clubbing and see someone and think, Oh, they're having the time of their life, they're really doing it. But the chances are they'd probably go home and the electricity would've run out or they'd have no money left for the rest of the week. It was always a front, but it was a very seductive front.'

So much for sex and drugs, then.

But what about Pulp?

ON FIRE AGAIN

WHAT about Pulp? Well, after his big move from Up North to Down South, Jarvis simply expected Pulp to 'cease to exist.'

That wasn't strictly the case, however. What happened was, by being less desperate to succeed, and by putting Pulp on the back burner, as it were, the group began to move at a more leisurely pace and achieve a certain slow momentum. Ironically, as soon as Pulp stopped taking an interest in what people thought of them, people started taking an interest in Pulp!

With Candida Doyle working in a toy shop, Russell Senior dealing in antique glass and Nick Banks teaching – all in Sheffield – and Jarvis and Pulp's umpteenth new bassist Steve Mackey (a student at the Royal College Of Art) down in London, the group started meeting roughly every month and playing the occasional gig.

In addition, Jarvis had those Fon tapes from his last days in Sheffield, with which he started shopping around for a one-single deal. Unfortunately, not one label agreed to sign – except, that is, for Fire, much to Jarvis' chagrin. Clearly, he hadn't yet forgotten how ineffectual they'd been regarding the promotion and distribution of his group's records.

So, throughout the Summer of 1989, Pulp started recording at Fon studios, on breaks from St Martin's and occasional weekends.

'Separations', their third album, was finished by Christmas. Trouble was, Fire refused to release it, despite Jarvis' protestations, although they did agree to put

out 'My Legendary Girlfriend' as a single in September 1990.

The electro-poppy 'My Legendary Girlfriend', which opened with one of Jarvis' trademark, husky, spoken, baritone monotone monologues, remains a live favourite with diehard Pulp fans. An *NME* Single Of The Week, it also won a special *Time Out* award for Best Five Minutes Of Simulated Sex for its heavy-breathing and

A (Silk) Cut above

'Je T'Aime'-style grunting (courtesy of Jarvis) and luscious sex rhythm (courtesy of Steve, Candida, Russell and Nick).

At last! They'd arrived! According to the singer, 'My Legendary Girlfriend' ushered in an exciting new era for Pulp, one 'where we actually started getting more, not less, popular.' Pulp were cool at last.

Story-wise, the single was, says Jarvis, 'about my girlfriend that I'd had in Sheffield while I was in London – I've never mixed business with pleasure, and I've always kept my private life separate from music. I've always gone out with girls who aren't interested in music, and so people kept asking me about my legendary girlfriend, because they'd never seen me with her.'

This might just be the Legendary Girlfriend with whom Jarvis discovered the guilty pleasure of smoking.

'I never really liked smoking,' he said, lighting a Silk Cut, 'and I got through my teenage years without ever having a fag. In fact, I used to really slag me mother off for smoking. And then I got to my early twenties and I was with this girl I was going out with at the time, and we were out one night and we were really bored, trying to think of something different to do, and we just thought, "Oooh, let's buy some cigarettes." We just thought it would be something interesting. So I bought a packet of 10 Consulates, and that was that – that was when I started to smoke.'

Meanwhile, Fire still hadn't released 'Separations'. By the summer of 1991, the label chose instead to put out another stirring, swirling disco drama of despair and disappointment, 'Countdown' ('About waiting for your life to take off'), as a single.

The last straw came after a double-blunder on the part of Fire: first, they refused to print Jarvis' sleevenotes for the 'Masters Of The Universe' compilation, and then they tried to release 'Separations' ('One of the great lost albums of the age' according to *Melody Maker*) on the same day as the brand new Pulp track, 'O.U.'

Pulp's days as indie's best kept secret were definitely numbered.

★★★★★★☆★☆★★★★★★

Razzmatazz

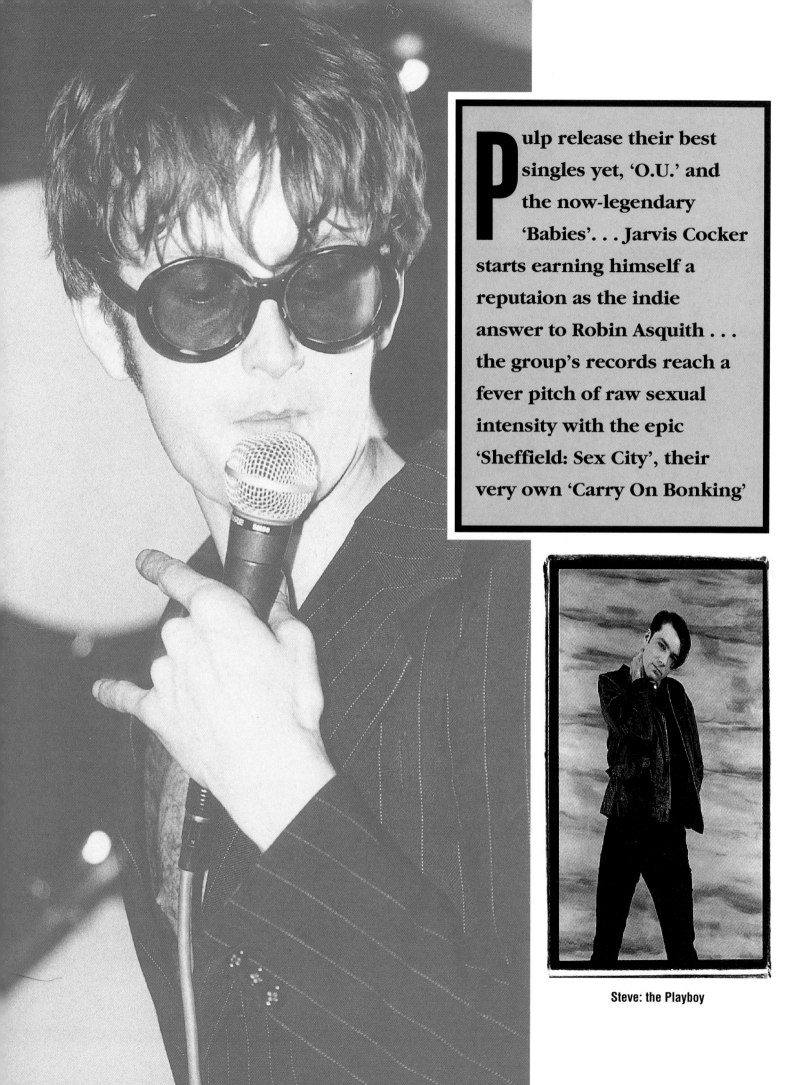

Pulp release their best singles yet, 'O.U.' and the now-legendary 'Babies'. . . Jarvis Cocker starts earning himself a reputaion as the indie answer to Robin Asquith . . . the group's records reach a fever pitch of raw sexual intensity with the epic 'Sheffield: Sex City', their very own 'Carry On Bonking'

Steve: the Playboy

INTRODUCING THE BAND

DURING 1992/3, Pulp recorded what was easily their best music thus far and released it on Gift Records, an independent Sheffield label run by the same people behind Warp, the home of such major Nineties electronica / ambient / techno figures as Aphex Twin, Black Dog and Autechre.

This is where Pulp finally started making the music for which they are now justly celebrated, their 'strangely affecting, swooping dramas on toy synthesisers, their futuristic space-pop about earthy emotions and ordinary lives' (Miranda Sawyer writing in *The Observer*).

This is also where you realise there is more to Pulp than Jarvis Cocker. Without Pulp, Jarvis would make a more than creditable space-age Tom Jones, crooning torch songs against some cheesy orchestral backdrop on the Rialto circuit or down at Barry Noble's Roxy, a sort of diseased, anorexic lounge lizard in crimplene Camdenwear, a surreally suave cabaret turn for the NW1 set.

But it's the other four members of Pulp who give Jarvis Cocker's glum bus-stop love stories and X-rated anecdotes an appropriately glam epic soundtrack, who give his comic bark a cosmic backing.

Nick Banks, Russell Senior and Steve Mackey supply the motorised/(Giorgio) Morodorised rhythm section and throbbing northern soul-cum-technopop basslines, while Candida Doyle provides the battery of Farfisas, Korgs, Stylophones and other synthesised relics which give Pulp their unique Seventies-cum-Nineties sound, a smashing clash of the kitsch and the colossal, the tacky and the titanic.

Pulp can be described, variously, as acrylic acid, dralon disco, terylene techno and formica funk. And their shuddering electronic depictions of Jarvis' melancholy bedsit melodramas are like New Order playing Nick Cave.

The three singles (plus superlative B-sides and extra songs) that Pulp made during this period – 'O.U.', 'Babies' and 'Razzmatazz' – are now available on the 'Pulpintro' collection, which was released by Island Records in 1993.

It could be reasonably argued that the nine tracks on 'Pulpintro' offer the most convincing justification yet for all the gushing praise drenched all over Pulp: this is no less than emotional, experimental, electronic music at its very, very best.

The first of the Gift singles was 'O.U.', a song ostensibly about train stations, but more probably about sex.

'Oh, the night was ending / He needed her undressed / He said he loved her / She tried to look impressed,' sang Jarvis, whooping, yelping and yeah-yeah-ing like a man possessed as the music built to an orgasmic peak of bubbling, squelching, fizzing synthesisers and clattering beats.

The *Melody Maker* reviewer, who made 'O.U.' Single Of The Week in May 1992, got appropriately carried away.

'This is three minutes of staggering

Russell: the Authoritarian

Nick: the Pre-Muncher

Candida: the Care-Bear

Pulp, about to ascend to . . .

popgasm,' he drooled, going on to praise 'the orchestra of organs, ascending chord sequence' and the way the singer braves 'the outer limits of desire. . . Jarvis Cocker's love life brims with the elation that comes with phenomenal doubt, pain and failure.'

COITUS 'R US!

THE second of Pulp's three Gift singles was the extremely catchy 'Babies'. Based around an infectious guitar motif, it is widely regarded by fans and critics alike as one of the group's finest moments.

MM spoke of 'budget magnificence. This is a blueprint for an epic to be constructed in a more liquid future. String arrangements are sketched in by synths, and, in lieu of the Royal Albert Hall, Jarvis has to make do with a deep-throat echo chamber.'

. . . the outer limits of desire

Basically, the song concerns a voyeuristic young lad who hides in his girlfriend's older sister's bedroom wardrobe and watches her having sex with *'some kid called David from the garage up the road'*. When the girl catches the teenage narrator the following day, she *'opens up the wardrobe'* and makes him 'get it on.' His excuse to his regular girlfriend? *'I only went with her cos she looks like you.'*

Not surprisingly, 'Babies' caught the attention of Island Records, one of the many major record companies who started pursuing Pulp around this time.

'We were still trapped in this legal minefield with Fire,' said Jarvis, 'but there were a lot of labels courting us – and it really was like courting. It's the nearest a bloke gets to being chatted up, being taken out to dinner and that stuff. All these people suddenly started taking notice.'

'Razzmatazz' was the third, and best, of the three Gift singles, its opening line – *'The trouble with your brother: he's always sleeping – with your mother'* – setting the scene for a bitter-sweet song with an exceptionally poignant melody and rousing chorus. It was another *Melody Maker* Single Of The Week, the paper unofficially making Pulp their cause *célèbre* of the early Nineties, preaching the gospel at every possible opportunity until the rest of the world eventually took notice.

Musically, the other tracks from this period showcased on 'Pulpintro' consist of pulsating 'Palitoy' beats interspersed with spooky interference from far-flung planets, kind of like intergalactic acid house performed by The Clangers and picked up by a long-range transmitter (see: 'Space', 'Styloroc [Nites Of Suburbia]'); and stomping Glitter rock with tidal wave choruses and glam handclaps ('Stacks').

Then there are the sex epics. '59, Lyndhurst Grove' is an atmospheric slice of queasy listening which details one of those dreadful, right-on, adult parties where all the grown-ups dance 'with children round their necks, talking business, books and records, art and sex'. 'Inside Susan: A Story In Three

Words-wise, anyone with a love of modern pop should already be familiar with the song's storyline – a rarity nowadays, when so many popsong so-called lyrics are regarded as almost surplus to requirements. 'Babies' is a splendidly sordid vignette which has been likened to 'an episode of *Grange Hill* directed by David Lynch' (*The Independent On Sunday*), a beautifully concise narrative, like a scuzzy little four-minute, BBC2-style *Play For Today* set to out-of-this-world space music.

Five Go Mad In London

Jarvis Cocker's vivid imagination. And there was no more telling example of how seriously people were beginning to take Pulp than the article in *The Independent On Sunday*, which said of 'Inside Susan': 'It's a psychological odyssey of greater depth and complexity than any previously attempted in British pop music.'

However, the real carnal *pièce de résistance* from this period was one of the extra tracks from the 'Babies' extended play – 'Sheffield: Sex City'.

'It's a bit crap,' said Jarvis, 'if you're so parochial that you're only allowed to write about humbugs and chippies. Sheffield may not be very sex, but then again, it is, because that was where I grew up, and where all my first sex was had.

'In Sheffield, when it's hot, you can feel the sap rising, and everything seems as if it's got something to do with sex, as if the whole city has sex on its brain.'

A massive, sprawling, absurd / awesome, eight-minute electronic tale of communal lust and urban meltdown, 'Sheffield: Sex City' is the track that really sealed Jarvis Cocker's reputation as the contemporary sex icon for student types and other assorted (and alienated) twentysomethings who don't have much luck with sex.

It starts with a soliloquy from Candida Doyle, overhearing her neighbours going at it hammer-and-tongs through the paper-thin bedroom walls (*'Have you ever heard other people fucking? It's not like in the movies'*). Then Jarvis reels off a list of placenames ('Wincobank, Crookes, Walkley, Broomhill') – which make Sheffield seem approximately five times as cool as New York, Los Angeles, Memphis, or any other of those typical locations from the lexicon of rock'n'roll – as the city is overcome with sex mania.

Finally, it builds towards a crescendo with loads of dogs copulating against streetlights and the narrator *'making love to all the cracks in the pavement'*, before the explosive climax where the whole of Sheffield reaches orgasm at precisely 4:13am (*'Everyone on Park Hill came in unison'*).

Astonishing.

Parts' follows the eponymous heroine from early adolescence to her early thirties, married to an architect somewhere in South London; it's a six-minute synth fable worthy of Mike Leigh, all *'sky-blue trainer bras'*, *'German exchange students who were very immature'* and other suburban trivia / memorabilia trawled from the depths of

★★★★★ ★★★★★★★★★★

Welcome To The New Era

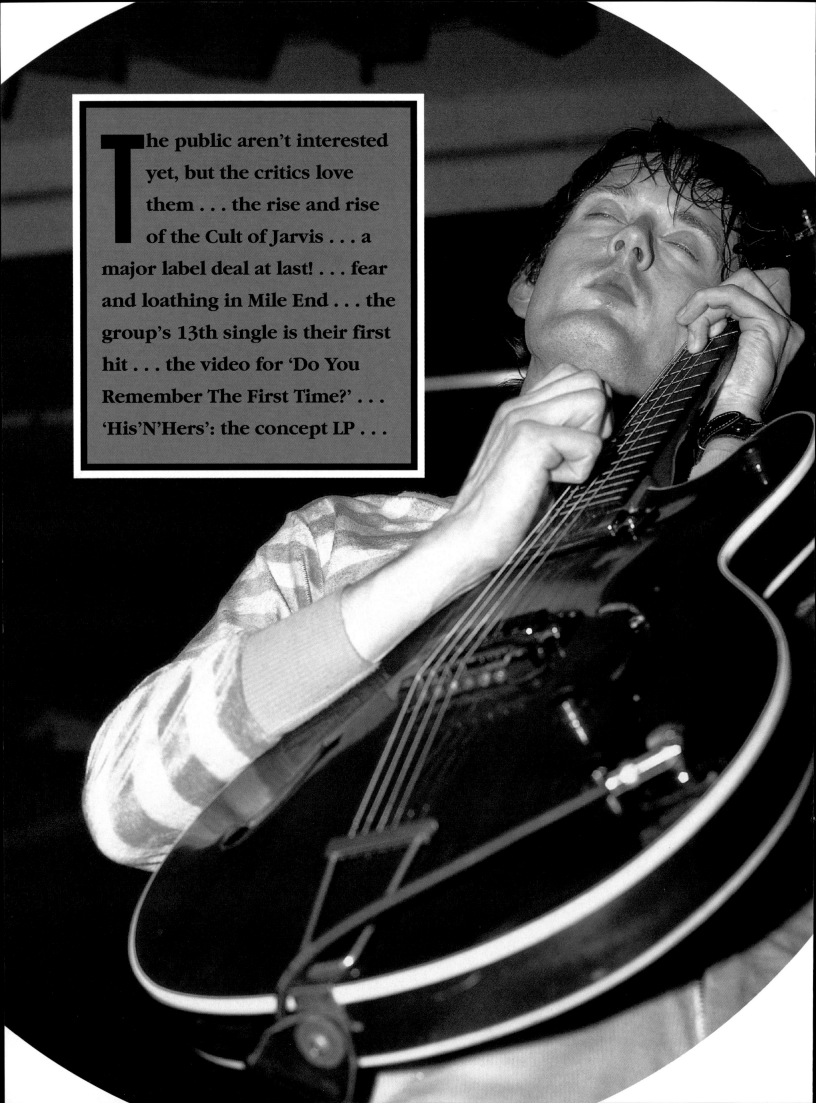

The public aren't interested yet, but the critics love them . . . the rise and rise of the Cult of Jarvis . . . a major label deal at last! . . . fear and loathing in Mile End . . . the group's 13th single is their first hit . . . the video for 'Do You Remember The First Time?' . . . 'His'N'Hers': the concept LP . . .

PRESS FOR ACTION

THE music papers, weeklies and monthlies, were going mad for Pulp by now.

'Every song is an exquisite, intricate melodrama skirting around social inadequcies and personal insecurities,' foamed *Melody Maker*'s Dave Simpson after witnessing the group live in Halifax, ending his review: 'This was one of the greatest pop performances I've ever seen.'

'Pulp are magic and Jarvis Cocker is a star,' beamed the *MM*'s Sharon O'Connell after a show at London's Subterania, adding: 'Pulp are not a bunch of cabaret clods with a fondness for the kitsch and the campily cute, they write damned fine pop songs which they deliver with a self-mocking sense of occasion. Monumentally groovy.'

'A fabulous mixture of the glamorous and the mundane,'

reckoned the same paper's Ian Watson. 'Pulp ought to be a national treasure. This is *Last Tango In Paris* set to a Europop beat,' reckoned Peter Paphides. Raved Simon Price: 'Pulp are a truly unique hybrid of Serge Gainsbourg sleaze, Northern Soul/soft-porn soundtrack, Farfisa organs and early Eighties New Romanticism (Soft Cell's 'Say Hello, Wave Goodbye', The Human League's 'Dare'). And they soar like nothing else this side of The Walker Brothers.'

Meanwhile, I managed to catch the group at The Dome in Tufnell Park and was able to make my own mind up.

'Pulp are Sheffield's greatest eccentric techno space-pop miserabilist cabaret troupe since The Human League,' I decided, 'a *Wheeltappers & Shunters* turn for the Ecstasy generation. Equal parts high camp and low rent, Pulp, like Morrissey, celebrate the serious facts and silly details of

Seventies British working-class life – star jumpers, *Look-In* annuals, tower blocks, feather cuts, and all.'

It was then that the other music weekly started to join in.

'We demand a real star,' opined the *NME*'s Angela Lewis. 'One with the spirit of Morrissey and Mark E Smith in his lyrics and that of Elvis Presley, Mick Jagger and James Brown in his hips. Jarvis Cocker, from Modestly Bonkers Street, Sheffield, will do. This is Seventies tackerama at its best. The cult of Jarvis is officially born.'

The cult of Jarvis was growing fast and furious. A series of articles in late 1992 and early 1993 keenly monitored the cult.

'We want to elevate everyday things to something exaggerated and exciting,' Jarvis told one keen reporter.

'Basically, all our songs are about either girls or space,' he told another. 'I like the

Pulp live = 'Seventies tackerama at its best'

The extremely funny Pulp relax

idea that Bri-Nylon was once going to be the fabric of the future. This fantastic, durable stuff rather than this rubbish that gave you a rash. Although the one-piece Bri-Nylon outfit never really took off in the way that the makers of *Space 1999* thought it would.'

'I like cooking,' he deadpanned his way through another intervew. 'Cooking for your friends is very therapeutic. And they always say it's nice 'cos they don't have to get out of their seats to help.'

And yet another: 'We might do a guide to the motorway service stations. There's a great Little Chef about half a mile down the road. And we're also hoping to get sponsored by Ginster's.'

Jarvis was on a roll by now, the (self) debunking one-liners pouring out of him: 'For about 10 minutes once, I actually thought I was Paul Nicholas.'

Stuart Maconie of the *New Musical Express* said it all: 'Pulp are one of the funniest groups I have ever met.'

ISLAND HOPPERS

SO the critics loved them. All Pulp needed now was for the general public to love them, too.

However, for the general public to agree with the nation's pop critics that Pulp were, indeed, the best thing since sliced Curly Wurly, they had to actually get to know about them first and hear them for themselves. Basically, Pulp needed the marketing, promotion and advertising muscle of a major label to get their music across to a wider audience, to get it into the shops and, ultimately, into as many homes as possible.

And so, in September 1993, and after more than a decade to-ing and fro-ing from one indie label to another, Pulp signed their lives away with Island, the multinational conglomerate responsible for, among many others, the biggest band on the planet – U2.

Jarvis Cocker remained utterly realistic about Pulp's chances in the market place, and refused to get carried away by all the 'what if?'s and 'maybe's.

'I understand the nature of a group's relationship with a record company,' he said at the time. 'I know that if we don't sell any records, we'll get dropped. But at least I feel as though we're working towards some kind of conclusion. At least we're going somewhere.'

After all the signing on the dotted line and champagne, Pulp now had to deliver their first record for a major label. That debut was 'Lipgloss'. It didn't disappoint.

Released in November '93, 'Lipgloss' came in a deliciously simple red-and-white pop art sleeve. The song was equally divine, three-and-a-half minutes of near-perfection, the sort of unimpeachable pop we hadn't heard from a Sheffield group, maybe any group, since ABC's 'Lexicon Of Love'.

For the lyrics to 'Lipgloss', Jarvis – who's into the idea of a tarnished, rather than perfect, glamour – described a scenario where a once-beautiful woman finds she's as unlucky in love as the next lipglossed siren (*'Nothing you do can turn him on / You had it once but now it's gone'*).

'Deep Fried In Kelvin' was one of two extra tracks available with 'Lipgloss', the other being a lugubrious ballad called 'You're A Nightmare', which was taken from Pulp's second Peel Session, from early '93).

Another 'Pulpintro'-style inner city epic, 'Deep Fried In Kelvin' is an extraordinary 10-minute slice of gritty social observation named after a monstrous sprawl of Sheffield tower blocks, one of those prize-winning blots on the horizon erected after the war. Imagine Phil Collins' underdog-friendly 'Another Day In Paradise', only good, or Marvin Gaye's 'Inner City Blues' remixed by Chicory Tip.

'Suffer the little children to come unto me,' intones the narrator at the start of the song, the messiah of South Yorkshire's council estates (curious fact: Jarvis Cocker has the same initials as the son of God). Meanwhile, the electronic pitter-patter, ominously rising chord sequence and simply affecting guitar pattern create a suitably apocalyptic musical backdrop.

'I will tend their adventure playground splinters and cigarette burns, and feed them fizzy orange and chips; that they may grow up straight and tall,' Jarvis carries on the recital with hymn-like gravitas, sounding as though he has been reincarnated as William Blake doing 'Jerusalem' to a disco beat.

Then, suddenly, you're struck with the impression of Jarvis as a kind of alternative Michael Jackson for dole queue girls and boys, all childlike empathy and Christlike feelings of benevolence towards the nation's youth.

Or maybe not.

Jarvis: the Morrissey You Can Dance To

THE LUXURY GAP

FOR all the excellence and increasingly lavish, expensive sound of Pulp's records, for all the praise and promise of riches, Jarvis was still living in London virtually like a pauper, several miles beneath the breadline, even after signing to Island Records. This may surprise some people who think that a major label record contract automatically spells penthouse suites, caviare and limousines.

Today, Jarvis lives in a fairly pleasant, fairly spacious flat in a fairly salubrious, leafy and trendily low-rent part of West London – Ladbroke Grove, to be precise, near the famous Portobello Road market.

Before that, though, he was in some grotty South London dreadzone between Camberwell and Peckham, which is where he had to stay first after his dramatic move down South. His next place of abode – and talk about downward mobility – was even worse, an East London hell-hole in Mile End (in fact, Pulp started playing a track called 'Mile End' around 1994/5 at concerts, although it has yet to appear on any Pulp record).

'When I moved down from Sheffield, I lived in a squat with Steve (Mackey),' he told this writer in 1995, 'which was something I never really pictured myself doing. I thought it was like a law that you had to have a mohican to live in a squat, and I couldn't really see me squatting in a corner, sniffing glue. It was kind of forced on us, though, because the flat we were supposed to have moved into fell through.

'Anyway, we soon got evicted from Camberwell, and we weren't aggressive enough to argue about it, so we went over to this tower block in Mile End that had a few spare places. It was only supposed to be a temporary measure, but we ended up spending nine months there which, without any question, were the worst nine months of my entire life.

'People go on about the East End, where everyone's friendly and you don't have to lock your door, but they were the most unfriendly people I've ever come across in my entire life. Like, you always got served last in the shop if they knew you weren't from around there. I never really got to know anybody who lived there – it's not like *Eastenders* at all.'

A couple of incidents recalled from this period when he was living in Hades, E15, still make Jarvis tremble…

'There was this pub up the road that we never used to go in where they used to play pool and it was, like, Winner Stays On,' he began his *Jackanory*-directed-by-Quentin Tarantino. 'Anyway, one night, this kid beat one of the regulars, who went off in a bit of a huff. Come closing time, we saw this bloke who lost the game of pool coming down the road with a shot gun. And this kid of about 17 ran over to warn his mate, and as he did, the bloke with the gun shot and killed him.

'So,' he concluded, and you could just tell it was black comedy bathos time, 'I was thinking of going in the pub the next night, plonking my 50p on the pool table and saying, "Winner stays alive!"'

Let's face it, the area was pretty grim. The 15th floor flat from hell didn't help.

'I was convinced that a murder had been carried out there,' he said, 'because there was all this mail for this one person, and because, all the time I lived there, the kitchen sink was blocked. It became an obsession to try and get it unblocked. And there was all this horrible stinky pink mushy stuff,

He knows what time it is

'Time for bed,' says Zebedee

together with this hydrochloric acid-type drain cleaner, and I started thinking that maybe the person living there before had killed his wife and then tried to dissolve her remains down the sink.

'It was horrible, because the bathroom sink was also broken, so I had to wash in a washing up bowl and I had to do all the washing up in the bath. That was what really summed things up for me: I was having a bath one day, lying low in the bath, as you do, and I suddenly saw this tomato skin floating on the surface of the water. I thought, "This is not how I want to live."'

So Ladbroke Grove must be a vast improvement on that.

'Yeah, it's much nicer round here. You can go out to a gig and come back late without being worried about getting shot.'

THE VIRGINIAN

PULP'S 13th single was lucky for them: it was their first ever Top 40 hit, reaching Number 33 in March 1994 – up to that point, 'Lipgloss' had been their closest brush with chart success, getting to Number 50 five months before. 'Do You Remember The First Time?' was Pulp's passport to pop's next level, the song that meant Jarvis' days of slumming it in sleazepits might just be coming to an end.

It was also the song that confirmed what we already suspected: Jarvis Cocker was Barry White in Barry Norman's body. The subject? Losing your virginity.

'I know you're going to let him bore your pants off . . . I don't care if you screw him just as long as you save a piece for me,' wailed Jarvis as Russell plucked a bassline half-inched from U2's 'I Still Haven't Found What I'm Looking For' and Candida drenched the whole thing in delectable, fizzing, frothy synth sounds and seagull noises.

'Do You Remember The First Time?' came backed with two extra tracks – the gorgeous 'Street Lites' and the complex, frantic/slow 'The Babysitter', featuring the character from 'Inside Susan' several years on – which were, if anything, even better than the title cut.

The Britpopracy (l-r): Sice of Boo Radleys, Jarvis, Louise Wener of Sleeper and Damon Albarn of Blur

Predictably, the *New Musical Express* and the *Melody Maker* both made it their Single Of The Week.

'"The Lexicon Of Love" updated,' said the former, while *MM* declared: 'Textually, Jarvis Cocker has invented his own distinctive magic realism, unlocking provincial England's humdrum epiphanies and neon romanticism.'

Spot on, that man.

VIDEO NICETY

THE single was accompanied by a now celebrated video. Instead of the usual pop promo where X band romp about pretending to be extras in some American slacker movie, bassist Steve Mackey and Jarvis, the latter by now a graduate with an upper-second-class, BA honours degree in film-making (he has since directed videos for

Tindersticks and Aphex Twin, among others), decided instead to make their very own 26-minute documentary about Doing It For The First Time.

The mini-documentary, also called *Do You Remember The First Time?*, was previewed at the Institute of Contemporary Arts in The Mall on a hot and humid night of 1000 stars, most of London's chi chi indie cognoscenti seemingly crammed into the capital's hippest venue to watch Pulp literally make sexual history.

For the film, Steve and Jarvis roped in a series of media types – Elastica's Justine Frischmann (Damon Albarn of Blur's missus), Vic Reeves and Bob Mortimer, former member of The Specials Terry Hall, comedienne Jo Brand, fashion designer Pam Hogg, actress Alison Steadman, John Peel –

then he got them to talk on camera about their very first sexual experiences, however harrowing, ludicrous or embarrassing.

In the by turns funny and touching film, Bob Mortimer recalled the feeling he had when he lost his virginity, an overwhelming feeling of, 'I'm about to do it, I'm doing it, I've done it.' Jo Brand remembered her head banging against the base of a toilet. Terry Hall sighed, 'She was very into the Bay City Rollers, which put me off a bit. But not enough.' And Jarvis himself disclosed that he did it outdoors in Weston Park near Sheffield University, a fact that he kept secret up till that point.

'Don't get me wrong,' said Jarvis after the film was broadcast on Channel 4, 'I'm not obsessed with sex.'

Yeah, right.

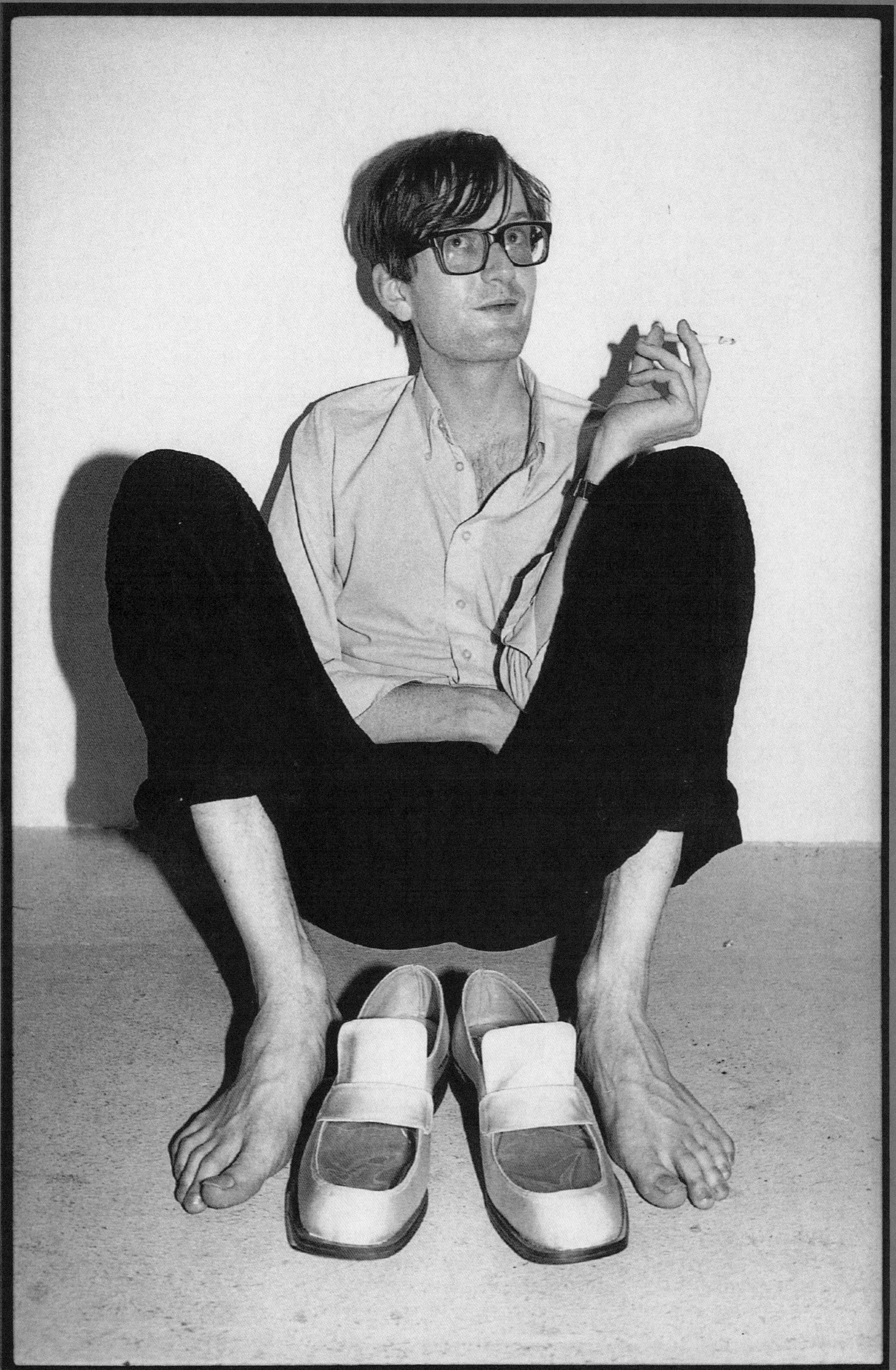

LET'S TALK ABOUT SEX (PG)

JARVIS Cocker is, as he has himself said, the only white pop artist currently addressing the subject of sex in an explicit manner. Historically, white pop sex has either been good, clean fun (see: The Beatles, The Beach Boys), its darker side has just been hinted at (The Rolling Stones, The Who), or it has been the cause of much angst (New Order, The Smiths).

Meanwhile, for today's black swingbeat artists, hip hoppers and G-Funkateers, sex is the mechanically precise variety, all domineering men and submissive women, gleaming musculature and cool biological fusion and fission.

Pulpsex is never the hygienic coupling you see all over the media, the seamless, juiceless, sexless, unproblematic sex we're all supposed to have as adults. No, Pulpsex is far more fumbling and fallible than that. This says plenty about the man responsible for writing about the sex (and the relationships and the one-night stands and the love and lust and frustration and desire and pleasure and pain) in Pulp's songs.

'There's always a tendency to hide the IQ when writing about sex,' said Jarvis, 'but I couldn't get away with writing about it like that, you know, the way Prince does, where you're at it all night long – I'd get the piss taken out of me, and rightly so.

'I can't do the macho thing,' he opened up. 'I'm not Mel Gibson. There's nothing in my psychological or physical make-up to enable me to do that kind of thing. I think all that bravado and bollocks that people talk down the pub is just crap. I wasn't brought up that way – there were no male figures in my childhood to base all that on. I was brought up in an extraordinarily female environment, which is probably why I write a lot of songs from a female perspective.'

A lot of women find that attractive, even sexy. In an interview with *The Face* around the time of the release of 'Do You Remember The First Time?', journalist Amy Raphael had this to say.

'With all his exaggerated physical freakiness, Jarvis has found himself a

Has he got shoes for you!

surprising pin-up. A friend of mine can't help herself when she sees him onstage. "My immediate reaction when I first saw him was, 'Yum, yum.' He's scrawny but very sexual. He's quirky. He's a poseur but he gets away with it. He knows what he's doing – he's not a 19-year-old playing around with an image he doesn't understand. I like men who dress up without being effeminate."'

As if to emphasise the last point, Jarvis turned up at another interview dressed in a knee-length fake fur coat, a tartan scarf, a tweedish jacket with leather detail, a shiny purple shirt, burgundy corduroys, pointed, stack-heeled, banana-coloured cowboy boots and outsized plastic-rimmed glasses.

'Well, I have always known I could never be sexy in a normal way. I haven't got the faculties. I wouldn't know I turned women on. I mean, I've got nice hands and nice fingers, but I'm really not so sure about the rest of me.

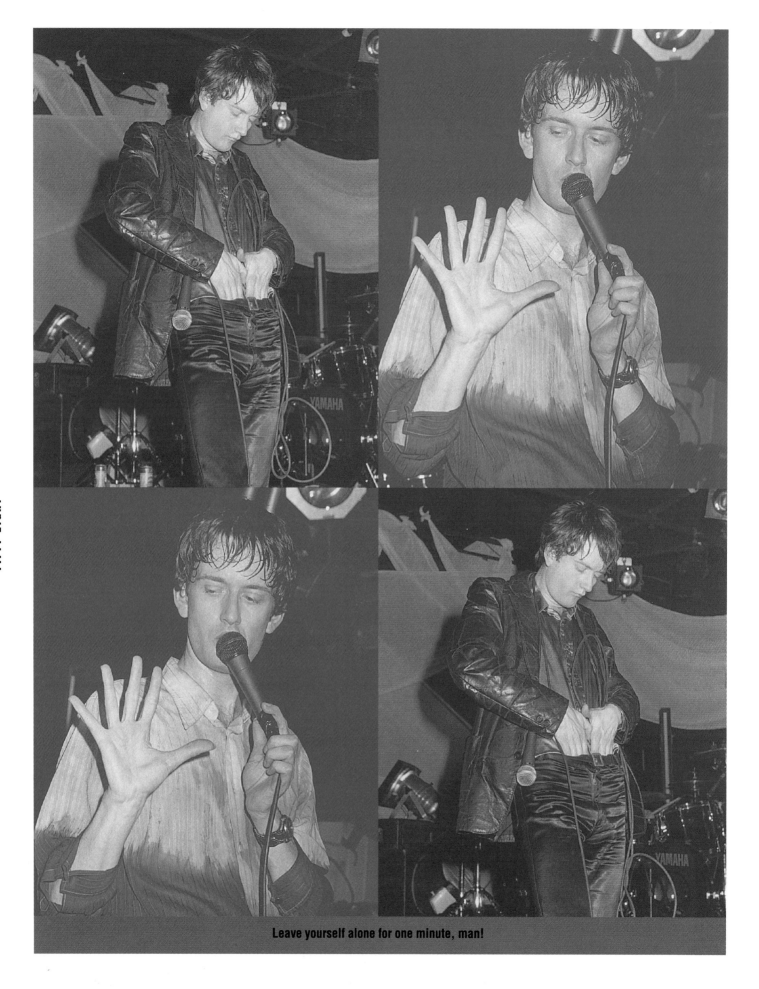

Leave yourself alone for one minute, man!

'Actually,' he decided, 'I would've said that the raw materials I was dealt at birth ha[d] me marked out for a *Blockbusters* contestan[t] – you know the type, slightly studious, wear[s] glasses, bit tall, bit of a stoop, go to university, get a job in a library. I've always considered it a mission to try and rise above that. In fact, I consider it a triumph if someone considers me attractive.'

LET'S TALK ABOUT SEX (18)

ALL this, of course, begs the question: is Jarvis Cocker obsessed with sex? Or are we just obsessed with the idea of Jarvis Cocker being obsessed with sex?

'I was speaking to our A&R (Artist & Repertoire) man at Island recently and he was asking me about our new songs,' Jarvis confided to me in 1995, 'so I told him, and he said, "They're all still about sex, aren't they?" And I said, Well, you know, I've got a one-track mind. I'm interested in sex. I like it. It's something which gets me excited. That's why I write about it. What do you want me to write about – knitting?

'I've been trying to think of something other than sex to be interested in,' he went on, 'but I'm not sure. I mean, it's a motivating force, isn't it? It's like, there's eating and there's reproducing – those are the two things that make people do things. There's nothing bigger in life.'

He added: 'I always thought of sex as something quite transcendental. Not that I'm into Tantric Sex, or anything, but I mean in the sense that it transcends. In a world where religion ceases to be a guiding force in people's lives, and apart from taking drugs, sex is the most important thing. That feeling you get at the point of orgasm is the most transcendental you can ever have.'

At the time of this interview, and at the time of writing this book, Jarvis was living with a girl called Sarah who worked at a mental health centre. I asked him how he reconciled the idea of the seedily exciting Pulp-type sex, the sort of sex celebrated in, say, 'Sheffield: Sex City', while in the confines of a stable relationship.

'I think it's good for sex to be an event,

His sexy moves, his deep croon, his flannel slacks . . .

and not always taking place in the same venue,' he hinted. 'It's better to go on tour. It's more exciting. Mind you, I'm not one of those people who has to think they might be discovered at any moment shagging in an alleyway, or wherever. Besides, you have to be pretty horny to do it in an alleyway, manhood-wise. Especially in Sheffield. Very cold up there, you know.

'But, yes, I do think that all the preamble and build-up is usually more exciting than actually doing it – that's when you can hardly contain yourself.

'I mean, the first time you touch somebody's hand can be the best thing ever. Can you recreate that every time with the same person? Depends if you live with them or if you see them that often. I thought that Woody Allen had the right idea – having separate houses that were near each other. It's all mental, though, I think. It takes effort, but I'm sure there is a way of living with someone and keeping it exciting.

'If you're in a steady relationship, it does kind of contradict the idea of sex as some kind of primal drive,' he generalised. 'It becomes something which is available, commonplace, and that can be a turn-off. You don't want sex to suddenly be timetabled – you know, like, go and buy the groceries, come back, indulge in 10 minutes of foreplay, have sex. You've got to try and keep it on a different plane, and that's difficult. I don't know if you can make the two sides of a relationship – companionship and sex – work together.'

Then again, I suggested, if Jarvis did finally sort out all of his various confusions about sex, then maybe he wouldn't write such great sex songs.

'I suppose if I started having a really successful sex life, I'd stop writing about it and concentrate on shagging! There's a theory that people create art because they're sublimating their sex desires in some way, or they have feelings of dissatisfaction which drive them to achieve certain things. So if you were really satisfied with sex, and life in general, you'd probably give up creating and get on with having a good time.

'But I wouldn't necessarily say I was having more successful sex nowadays. I might be having more of it, but I don't know if it's more successful. It depends how you measure sex. I mean, there isn't a score-card in operation.'

I told Jarvis that I once dubbed Pulp 'The Smiths You Can Have Sex To', while he was 'Morrissey With A Groin'. Then I asked him whether, in this era of the New Lad, it was finally considered all right to admit to admiring the female form.

'Well, it's nicer to look at than the male form, isn't it? And I think that women would agree with that as well. It's just that the shape of it is more balanced, because it's got a nice curve to it, and you've got the breasts which balance the bottom part. You can have good-looking men as well, I suppose. But a woman's sexual parts are much nicer-looking than a man's.'

Talking of lads . . .

'It can be quite funny, that laddish thing,' he said, suddenly nostalgic. 'Like the lads at school – they were always doing stupid things like spraying "Welcome To Colditz" on the school wall and then getting caught and having to scrub it off. And lads do have some good jokes. Like, when my sister was about 15 and she'd just been to the chip shop and she was walking back, eating her chips, and this gang of lads were going, "Oy, do you want a sausage with them chips, love?" It's just daft.'

Isn't it offensive?

'It really depends how you've been brought up. It's like, sometimes you don't actually know the meaning of words. It's like the way they use the word "nigger" all the time in that film *Pulp Fiction*. Or, like, when you're at school you might say, "Come here, you spaz." At our school, it was just the same as calling somone a "git" or a "tit". You weren't actually saying that you thought that person was disabled. It's only when you get older that you come to realise how offensive it might be.

'I mean, I get offended sometimes. I have a strict moral code. I think there's such a thing as right and wrong. For example, I

. . .Yes! Jarvis Cocker is the Nineties Tom Jones

Going for that James Bond look

thought it was wrong that, after the Hillsborough disaster, there were all these gruesome images of it in the papers. I thought that was really offensive. I also get offended if people come out with racist remarks. That can really put you off a person.'

I guided the subject back to sex and asked Jarvis whether he had broadly conventional tastes in women?

'You mean towny lasses? Yeah, they're all right,' he answered in a very matter-of-fact way. 'But I hate all that Ann Summers thing, supposedly erotic lingerie where it's, like, black polyester satin with synthetic red trim and synthetic lace. Although there is one shop I keep meaning to go to that's just opened up in Soho which sells rather more demurely sexual things.'

Ironically, some people have described Jarvis as effeminate, even androgynous.

'I'm not androgynous, it's just that I'm not macho and could never be. But I do like taking care of my appearance. Not that I'm

into designer labels or anything like some people are – "Oh, you're wearing Versace tonight." But I like well-made clothes – and that's not unmasculine.

'Then again, you shouldn't judge people by their clothes. I'm not bothered what people are wearing when I talk to them, I only care whether they're boring or interesting. I used to go to this club in Sheffield called The Limit, and all the men wore eyeliner and I thought they looked interesting, but they weren't. After that, I always thought anybody that looked interesting but who actually bored the pants off you should be prosecuted under the Trade Descriptions Act.'

Has Jarvis, I wondered, ever had a close encounter of the homosexual kind?

'Never. I'm as straight as a die. Not that I think that's anything to be particularly proud of. I can appreciate that some men look nice, but the truth, is I've never had any inclinations that way.'

HIS 'N' HERSTORY

THERE was plenty of sex on 'His 'N' Hers'.

Released in April 1994 and reaching Number Nine in the charts, this was Pulp's fourth LP, their first for Island Records and the one that many people refer to now as the group's debut album.

It wasn't all about sex, though. Jarvis did tackle other subjects on 'His 'N' Hers'. For example, there was the opening track, 'Joyriders', with its hilarious / horrible lyric, one that expressed Cocker's ambiguous feelings towards the sort of casual-dressed, working-class bootboys you see in every town centre – a combination of sheer loathing and utter fascination.

'Hey, you, in the Jesus sandals / Would you like to come / Over and watch some vandals / Smashing up someone's car / We can't help it, we're so thick / We can't think of anything 'cept shit, sleep and drink.'

According to Jarvis, 'Joyriders' was a gang-banging exaggeration of a real-life encounter between himself and a group of thugs that he chanced upon one day when his decrepit old Hillman Imp broke down.

Even 'Joyriders' was, eventually, about sex, albeit the most repulsive variety (the yobs in the song, if not the ones that Jarvis met on that fateful day, were on their way to a reservoir with a girl, intending either to rape her or to bury her).

Get right down to it, all the songs on 'His 'N' Hers' were about shagging; 'little kitsch'n'sink dramas about urban deprivation and strange sex' (*The Sunday Times*), equal parts disco fantasy and dismal reality, both *Saturday Night Fever* and *Saturday Night And Sunday Morning*.

Apart from 'Lipgloss', 'Babies' and 'Do You Remember The First Time', which we already knew, there was 'Acrylic Afternoons' (*'I want to pull your knickers down'*); 'Have You Seen Her Lately?', where the female character needs to escape a claustrophobic relationship (*'First you let him in your bed /*

Very suave

He's not always suave, though

Now he's moved inside your head'); the tangled web of intrigue and deceit that was 'She's A Lady' (a musical echo of disco classic 'I Will Survive'), where the 'hero' two-times his girlfriend with an insatiable older woman who sells revealing photos of her to German businessmen; 'Happy Endings' ('The aftermath of our affair is lying all around / And I can't clear it away'); and 'Pink Glove', where the boy doesn't care what the girl wears, 'Just as long as it's pink and tight.'

Make no mistake about it, 'His 'N' Hers' was Whatever Happened To The Likely Lads meets the Kama Sutra, with guitars and a pulsing techno beat.

Jarvis explained the theme of the record at the time of its release, how his often jaundiced view of relationships were formed when he was very young and his mother, his Aunty Mandy and their friends used to have 'all these parties' after their husbands had 'long since pissed off.'

'There would be all these people snogging on the stairs,' he recalled, explaining how it helped put him off marriage for life because he'd never seen any examples of couples actually staying together.

'His 'N' Hers' is about that dreaded concept – The Couple.

'Yeah, it's mostly about how, if you get into a relationship, you subjugate parts of your personality. It's that thing where two people start wearing matching clothes, their personalities start to merge, they know exactly what each other's thinking, and they haven't a whole personality of their own any more. They've just got half of someone else's. If that relationship breaks down, you're suddenly an incomplete person.'

The mission statement on the back cover of 'His 'N' Hers', spelled out nice and simply in big, bold, red capital letters, neatly summed up Jarvis' attitude.

'Please deliver us from matching sweatshirts and "chicken in the rough", from evenings sat on couple row admiring the flock, from Sundays spent parading the aisles of Meadowhall. We don't want to live like this. It's bad for our health. Do something soon or it's curtains (just as long as they match with the walls and the sofa).'

Masters Of The Universe

FILM FESTIVAL
PULP (pulp) n.
1. A soft, moist,
shapeless mass
of matter.
2. A book contain-
ing lurid subject
matter, and
being charac-
teristically
printed on
rough,
unfinished
paper.

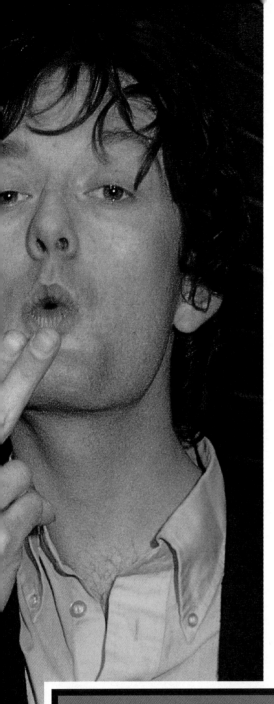

UPWARDS AND ONWARDS

AFTER 'His 'N' Hers', Pulp released 'The Sisters EP'. It featured 'Babies', made available once more after public demand, plus three extra tracks from the 'His 'N' Hers' LP sessions: 'Your Sister's Clothes' ('The sisters from "Babies" four years on'), 'Seconds', and a song called 'His 'N' Hers' which was like a cross between Hot Butter's early Seventies novelty synthi-ditty, 'Popcorn', Chicory Tip's 'Son Of Your Father' and 'Magic Fly' by Space.

All three bonus tracks were well worth hearing, as per usual, and the EP climbed to the Number 19 slot in the charts in May 1994. This was easily Pulp's biggest hit single to date, which meant the group were invited to appear on *Top Of The Pops* for the first time, the realisation of one of Jarvis' main childhood ambitions.

Jarvis celebrated this momentous occasion in inimitably awkward style, outrageously opening his jacket in front of 10 million BBC1 viewers to reveal an 'I Hate Wet Wet Wet' sign stuck inside! (the Wets had virtually monopolised the top slot that year with their anodyne version of the ancient Troggs hit featured in the film *Four Weddings And A Funeral* – the irritatingly ubiquitous 'Love Is All Around').

'I always hated Wet Wet Wet,' he told *Melody Maker*, 'ever since their first single. I thought they were one of the worst groups in the world. It's Marti Pellow's smirk, I suppose. When I found out that *Top Of The Pops* was going to be broadcast live, I thought that if I didn't do something to surprise the powers that be, even if it meant we'd get banned from the show for all time, I'd never forgive myself.

'I got a letter just the other day from this irate Wet Wet Wet fan, actually,' he added, clearly proud of the fact, 'the first line of which was "Dear Bastard." Which I thought was a great opener.'

The next step on the road towards total mainstream recognition for Pulp and Jarvis Cocker came when 'His 'N' Hers' was nominated for 1994's prestigious Mercury Music Prize alongside the likes of Blur, The Prodigy and Paul Weller. Out of the dozen candidates, Pulp came in second, reportedly losing the £25,000 prize to pop-soul band M-People by just one vote.

'They're terrible,' Jarvis said later, not being one to bear a grudge. 'I mean, aside from the fact that we needed the money and they didn't . . . What I hate about M-People most of all is the feeling that they really think that there's some kind of "quality" in what they do, when really it's just complete blandness. I love disco music and that, but I like stuff like Whigfield, where it's just a pop song and it's not trying to be anything else.

'Anyway, we just kept out their way that night. I saw that woman with the pineapple on her head go past,' he refers to M-People's glamorous chanteuse with the gravity-defying haircut, 'and I just looked in the opposite direction. Later, I was particularly violent towards a fruit bowl.'

Ironically, 'His 'N' Hers' also got pipped to the post in the *Melody Maker* end of year critics' poll, this time by Portishead's trip hop masterpiece, 'Dummy' – which won 1995's Mercury Music Prize.

Pulp rounded off their best year so far by playing a version of Urge Overkill's take on MOR king Neil Diamond's 'Girl You'll Be A Woman Soon', from cult movie *Pulp Fiction*, at a party for director Quentin Tarantino.

Pulp on *Top Of The Pops* . . . a Mercury Music Prize nomination . . . Jarvis at the Brits . . . the group go supernova with 'Common People' . . . television ubiquity: *The Big Breakfast, Dear Dilemma, Shooting Stars* . . . introducing the band . . . the great 'Es and Whizz' controversy . . . the album 'Different Class' establishes Pulp as a national institution . . .

And Jarvis rounded off his best year so far by appearing on a now legendary edition of *Pop Quiz*, on which he showed up team-mates and ex-celebrities Des'ree and Chesney Hawkes, trashed the opposition with his encyclopaedic pop knowledge, and proved that he was a TV personality just waiting to be given his own chat show.

How did Jarvis, a mixture of the earthy and the effete, the coarse and the camp, remember this slice of telly history?

'I was too pissed to notice, really.'

FANFARE FOR THE 'COMMON' MAN

AND then, in June 1995, Pulp released 'Common People' and they went supernova.

'Common People' was a staggering piece of synthesised pop invective that related the story of a spoilt little rich girl of the singer's acquaintance, from his St Martin's days; a student from a wealthy Greek family who wanted to take a brief, vicarious holiday in other people's misery by slumming it for a while, moving into a scuzzy, low-rent neighbourhood, shopping in scummy grocers and sleeping with, as she put it to Jarvis at the time, 'common people'.

Musically, 'Common People' was anthemic, gigantic, its relentlessly intense rhythm and motorcading pace recalling the demonic, supersonic, electronic mo-mo-momentum of Brian Eno-era Roxy Music (something like 'Street Life' or 'Virginia Plain', say). Meanwhile, the song's juggernaut keyboard riff and vitriolic sex-geek lyric smacked of Elvis Costello at his most bitter and twisted, in the era of 'I Don't Want To Go To Chelsea'.

The B-side, 'Underwear', was a spacey mood ballad about stripping off, reaching the point of no return with a one-night stand and seeing your new partner in their underwear for the first time.

'It's about how, once you've taken off somebody's clothes, it's hard to put them back on and leave and just say, "Sorry, I didn't actually mean it."'

Jarvis took the opportunity to reveal his own underwear habits to the world.

'I don't wear any,' he said, without a

Jarv, surrounded by babes, as usual

'And the winners are . . . Pulp!'

moment's hesitation. 'Or, at least, I never used to. I sometimes do now. I hate boxer shorts – they're crap. I don't see the point in them – there's no support. If you run, it's all flopping about. I prefer the trunks type – not with the legging, but kind of like Y-fronts. You can get them from Marks & Spencer in three-packs. I have tangas as well, but they're disgusting, really tiny.'

Now you know.

The single entered the charts at Number Two, and although it was kept off pole position by a granny-friendly cover of The Righteous Brothers' 'Unchained Melody', it also managed to keep the biggest star in the cosmos, Michael Jackson, at Number Three, with his comeback single, 'Scream'.

Suddenly, Pulp were as ubiquitous as Wet Wet Wet. The group performed on *Alive And Kicking*, Jarvis hosted *Top Of The Pops* again (when he gently ridiculed all the other artists) and presented an award at the Brits.

'There were all these people in these Portakabins backstage like Elton John and Sting. I went to the toilet and suddenly realised I was pissing next to Tom Jones! He had his cock out in the little urinal next to me.'

Jarvis got beaten up quite badly the Christmas before last after a party in Islington ('I had to go to hospital and everything'). Despite incidents like this, he can't ever envisage a time when he might use personal bodyguards, just like all the megastars at the Brits did.

'No, I can't understand that. It's so stupid. People like Madonna and Prince get really famous, then they suddenly decide, "Right, I'm not going to have anything to do with anyone else, and when I walk about, I'm going to have 10 bodyguards with me." What a boring life! You never get to meet anyone. What kind of danger are you in at something like the Brits? I mean, Terence Trent D'Arby's hardly going to just suddenly Ninja you, is he?'

Groovy

Then he appeared on Channel 4's *The Big Breakfast* for the second time, BBC2's *Dear Dilemma* and Reeves & Mortimer's *Shooting Stars*, as well as the cover of *Top Of The Pops* magazine with none other than Kylie Minogue ('She made me quite nervous. But then, people are sometimes nervous of me').

All this and he even got described by *Smash Hits* magazine as 'one of the biggest pop stars in Britain.'

'It's important to go on those things and not be a cheesemaster,' he said of his numerous cool TV appearances. 'I mean, people say to me: "Why don't you go on those programmes with your cock out and say 'f*** off' and do a dump." But that's just immature and stupid. That kind of rebellious, I'm-not-going-to-do-what-my-parents-tell-me-to behaviour just isn't rebellious any more.'

I asked Jarvis how he felt about his new-found fame and its accoutrements.

'Well, apart from anything else, this is definitely the most comfortable position I've ever been in, especially compared to 10 years on the dole. I'm not loaded with money, or anything, but I've got more than I had. I mean, five years ago I might have been getting in a flap about whether or not to put the second bar on the fire.'

Jarv has a *Big Breakfast*

In November 1995, Jarvis told *Q* magazine that he was thinking of getting some cards printed that say, 'Yes, I am', for all the people who stare at him in the street, wondering if it really is The Famous Jarvis Cocker From Pulp. He even went on holiday to Iceland at the end of last year (where he stayed at Bjork's house! – 'My flat would have fit in it six times') to get away from it all.

Would he ever be prone to the sorts of

pressures that led Kurt Cobain to kill himself, or The Manic Street Peachers' Richey James Edwards to disappear without trace?

'I would if I'd have had a bit more success when I was younger,' he said. 'But because it's taken such a long time, and I've done so many other things, I don't think I would be now. Because I know there's always another world, always other things to do, a way out. There are other things apart from music that

you can do – like be a gardener.

'I also know enough to realise the reality of pop success isn't quite what you might imagine it to be. You build up a picture in your mind of what it's all about. Like, you can be having a shit one day, thinking, "If only I was a pop star, I'd be so happy, I'd get all the birds I want, everyone would think I'm great, I'd be able to get into all these places for free, and life would be totally sorted."

'But it's not like that at all.'

FANFARE FOR THE 'COMMON' BAND

THE other members of Pulp are just as down-to-earth as Jarvis Cocker. In fact, there was a Pulp fanzine in the late Eighties that offered cartoon definitions of Russell Senior (the stern, authoritarian one), Candida Doyle (the fluffy, pretty, friendly one), Steve Mackey (the suave ladykiller) and Nick Banks (the bluff, cheery fan of beer and pies).

Russell was born in Sheffield in 1961, and graduated from Bath University with a degree in Business Studies the year before he joined Pulp. He's one of only two Pulp-ers to have stayed in Sheffield, where he lives with his girlfriend and children.

His musical influences are Eastern European folk, electronic post-punk duo,

Suicide, Kraftwerk, The Rolling Stones and classical composer Bach. His favourite singles are Clock DVA's 'Four Hours' and The Sex Pistols' 'Pretty Vacant', and favourite albums are Clock DVA's 'Thirst' and St Etienne's 'Foxbase Alpha'. Senior seems to have mellowed somewhat since the disciplinarian phase for which he was previously renowned ('I used to wake everyone up in the morning'), and which earned him comparisons with the poker-faced Ron Mael, he of the Hitler moustache, from Seventies quirky-pop twosome, Sparks. But he's still pretty hardline when it comes to his assessment of Pulp, the group he's been with for 12 years.

'I'd say that, if Blur are The Beatles of this Britpop thing, then we, not Oasis, are The Rolling Stones,' he told me last year. 'There's a dark edge to what we do that I've always thought was quite Stones-y. Not that we've ever slaughtered anything sacrificial' A lot of people haven't really paid much attention to this aspect of the group, though, because they've been too busy looking at what they think is the band's kitsch side. But that's just the way Jarvis dresses.

'I'd like to push the dark side of Pulp. It's always been there, especially on the first few

Bjork and Jarv

Russell: 'I'm very poor'

Mind you, even if we did have more money, we'd still shop at Oxfam.'

Candida Mary Doyle was born in Belfast on August 25th, 1963, and educated at St Andrews school in Sheffield. Her favourite singles are Bill Withers' soft-soul classic, 'Lovely Day' and The Undertones' 'Get Over You', while, album-wise, she likes Spiritualized's 'Lazer Guided Melodies', Love's 'Forever Changes', Pink Floyd's 'Piper At The Gates Of Dawn' and the 'Don't Walk, Boogie' disco compilation.

Until recently, Candida still lived in Meersbrook, Sheffield, with her long-term boyfriend (with whom she reportedly lost her virginity a decade before). When I interviewed her last year, she had moved to Stoke Newington, in North London, but was already considering moving again, maybe back up north to Sheffield.

Candida: 'I can be laddish'

Steve: 'I drink a lot of tea'

albums. I can't listen to those anymore – they're too bloody dark for me! But I actually think the new stuff is even darker. We can be celebratory in terms of our musical moods at times, but that doesn't mean we have to write something like The Boo Radleys' 'Wake Up Boo!' We're not about false optimism. Our world is quite grainy and black and white, with weird things in it, but what the hell, let's dance.'

Russell explained that, despite Pulp's increasing success, he was still hardly what you might call finanically secure.

'I'm very, very poor,' he admitted. 'Do you want to know how poor? Well, two weeks ago, I really wanted to go to Scarborough for the weekend, but I couldn't afford it. We're all spectacularly poor, actually. All bands are a lot poorer than you might think, actually.

'Me and my boyfriend were on this boat in Regents Park and he said, "Why don't we move to London?" and I said, OK. And after three months we thought, Why have we done this? In the last six years, I've moved every year, so . . . I always thought London would be like that book, *London Belongs To Me*, where the girl walks around Trafalgar Square and it's nice and sunny. It was at first, when we moved down. Then it's just like anywhere – having to do the shopping and all that stuff.'

How, I wondered, was Candida coping with their success?

'It's really good at the moment,' she told me. 'I find it easier now. I used to hate photo sessions and interviews. I'd have to get really pissed. Now I find it quite relaxing.

'I never thought we'd be this big, you

know,' she confided. 'But I want us to get bigger now. I want to make loads of money! What would I do with it? The problem wouldn't be spending it, because I save money like mad. I always feel really bad when I spend it. That's what I do: I save, then I spend hundreds. But I'm quite tight when it comes to money. I've always been really bad when it comes to tipping.

'I get recognised quite a lot these days, especially when I'm back in Sheffield,' she went on. 'I went to the Abbey National the other day, and I had to show my passport, and they all came over and said, "We don't really need to ask you who you are – you're Candida from Pulp, aren't you?" Then I was in The Crucible (famous Sheffield theatre) and they put on "His 'N' Hers" and I thought, Christ. I couldn't believe it. Sometimes, being in Pulp, I feel like I'm drunk or on

Pulp: The Smiths with synthesizers

Nick: 'I never count my chickens'

drugs, really unreal, kind of dizzy.'

What's it like being the only female in Pulp?

'I always feel like I'm in the middle, being the only girl. Actually, it used to be more of a North versus South thing, with me, Russell and Nick still back in Sheffield, and Jarvis and Steve living in London. I kind of swop between cliques.

'Can they be laddish? Well, it's hardly like Oasis! I can be a bit laddish as well, you know. I think if I was in a group with five girls it'd get a bit annoying. I've only lost my temper once: we were on tour and we were in this really horrible, dark, small dressing room and there was graffitti everywhere, and Nick had this *Sun* newspaper and he was going, "Phwoarrgghh!!" And I just went and grabbed it and chucked it in the bin. I think he found it quite funny.

'Some people find me quite, well, not scary, but stand-offish.'

Stephen Patrick Mackey, the 'new boy' in Pulp, was born in Sheffield on November 10th, 1966, and used to be an advice worker before entering the Royal College Of Art where he studied film-making for seven

years. His main musical influences are Scott Walker, electro / disco pioneer Giorgio Moroder, the composer Burt Bacharach, techno pioneer Derrick May, St Etienne, Nick Cave and movie soundtrack king John Barry.

Unlike Russell and Nick, Steve – who bears a striking resemblance to Alex James, the bassist with Blur – was not in a steady relationship at the time of writing ('I'm the joker in the pack'). He had also just moved into a flat with Justin Welch, the drummer for Britpop peers, Elastica.

'We drink a lot of tea and watch telly,' he said. 'That's about as wild as it gets.'

Steve explained that Pulp were finally starting to sound like the group he'd always wanted to be in.

'For the first time ever, we sound right, exactly how we want to sound. We're a lot more focused now. I mean, I always thought Pulp were good. We've never moved with any fads, and no one's ever been able to pin us down to one style or movement or set of musical references.

'In fact, in terms of the instrumentation we use, our emotional impact, our

The return of skinny-tie Power Pop?

glamorous presentation and sonic experimentation, I'd say that, if anyone, we were like Roxy Music.'

Nicholas David Banks was born in Rotherham in 1965 and educated at Sheffield's Oakwood Comprehensive. His musical influences are disco, punk, Jonathan Richman's 'Roadrunner' and Jonathan King's 'Everyone's Gone To The Moon', Prefab Sprout and Primal Scream.

Before joining Pulp, Nick was employed as a wreath-maker in Sheffield. He didn't go

along with the idea that Pulp are, in any way at all, related to those other Sheffield bands of the early Eighties – ABC, The Human League and Heaven 17.

'Not at all,' he said. 'People have often compared us to Soft Cell. Now, I must admit, Soft Cell are one of the worst groups of all time. I would gladly go and shoot Marc Almond. When I was a kid, all my mates would play "Tainted Love" non-stop. I hated it straight away – I can't be doing with it.'

Banks admitted he was delighted with

Pulp's success, because, whereas before his family would say, 'Bloody get a job, you've been loafing around the house doing nothing,' now they have seen him on *Top Of The Pops* and realise he's actually doing something valid with his life.

Not that he would ever let Pulp's current fame and fortune go to his head: 'I never count my chickens. Some bands give up really quickly, whereas we just plod along. Hopefully, we're still moving upwards. We haven't reached our peak yet.'

SORTED

NO chance. In June 1995, Pulp were headliners at the Glastonbury Festival, replacing The Stone Roses, who dropped out at the last minute. It was a defining moment of the Britpop era, and everyone who was there agreed that it was more than Pulp's finest hour, it was one of those great, historic performances, the likes of which you only witness once or twice a decade.

Jarvis Cocker was equally overawed.

'I was crapping myself,' he told John Peel. 'Beforehand, I had to hold onto the arms of this chair – I thought I was going to fall off and have an accident. I wasn't thinking rationally. But it was OK once we went on, mind.'

In July, Pulp headlined Leeds' Heineken Festival, re-named 'Britstock'.

'Pulp are the non-surprise hit of the festival, four weeks after being the surprise hit of Glastonbury,' I wrote at the time. 'Pulp are reaching critical mass right now. There are times during their set when they induce

Jarv in best festival wear

Jarvis slays 'em at Glastonbury

Jarvis being interviewed at Glastonbury, with (right) new recruit guitarist Mark Webber who made his album debut on 'Different Class'

Not behind bars. Yet

the sort of communal awe I have only experienced this decade in Glasgow (Kraftwerk), Mile End (Blur), Sheffield (Oasis), Manchester (Public Enemy) and Munich ("Zooropa").

'Pulp are "our" U2,' I raved on, 'playing with electronics, playing with video, playing with humour, playing with time.'

And then, in the modest words of Nick Banks, Pulp 'plodded on' towards pop's summit in October when they put out their follow-up to 'Common People', the double A-side single, 'Mis-Shapes'/'Sorted For E's And Wizz' (not forgetting the superb extra track, 'P.T.A.'). Both songs were as brilliantly catchy and anthemic as their predecessor, the former a sort of 'All You Need Is Love' for the Ecstasy/rave generation, the latter a typically cautionary tale from Jarvis Cocker's Acid House period.

In fact, the subject matter of 'Sorted For E's And Wizz' led to a bit of a kerfuffle when

the *Daily Mirror* put Pulp on the front page of their September 20th edition, with the headline, 'Ban This Sick Stunt'.

The cover of the single featured a photograph of a page of a magazine folded into the shape of a speed wrap, although no drugs were shown on the sleeve. And the inside booklet featured a series of origami-style diagrams showing how to fold a piece of paper to make a speed wrap. Under pressure from the tabloids, record retailers and Island Records, a new, plain white sleeve was printed up at the last minute.

'Chart stars sell CD with DIY kids' drugs guide,' screamed the *Daily Mirror*, although, in the following day's edition, Jarvis made sure he set the record straight.

'"Sorted For E's And Wizz" is not a pro-drugs song,' he said. 'I wouldn't want anything we do to encourage people to take drugs because they aren't a solution or an answer to anything. That song is just a factual account of something that happened to me in 1989 when I first moved to London and the rave scene was really big. I went to these raves and I tried E's and speed during the summer. After a while, though, I became disenchanted with it all.

'I have the knowledge of taking drugs first hand. But I also fell out of a window once when I was drunk, and I wouldn't try to offer advice on that, either.'

Jarvis spoke to *Melody Maker* the same week as all the tabloid furore, and was suitably perplexed by the whole thing: 'It's stupid, because it (the speed wrap picture) was basically just an origami diagram. Origami does not lead to drug addiction, as far as I know. But I could be wrong. Nowhere on the sleeve does it say: "Put your drugs in this handy container."

'To me, it's a really inoffensive song. It's about that horrible feeling when you've had a great time and the next morning reality starts to seep in and you're left with this hollow feeling and your brain feels like a pea rattling around in a shoe box. There's the worry that you've done yourself some permanent damage and you're never gonna be able to get back to normal again.'

Added Jarvis: 'I'm quite into the fact that all this has given the record lots of publicity, but I'm not looking forward to going through customs next time. I'll probably have a

Pulp pervert the nation's youth

Sure, Jarvis, we believe you

vacuum cleaner shoved up my arse.

Finally, he joked that the title of Pulp's next single was going to be, 'Heroin Is Great'.

None of this stopped the single doing extremely well, of course. Pre-sales orders for the single were already well over 200,000 before its release – the biggest advance figure in the history of Island Records, according to the label's marketing director – and it finally entered the UK charts in the first week of October at Number Two, kept off the top slot this time by the mega-selling single, 'Fairground', by the 'housewives choice', Simply Red.

UPPER 'CLASS'

PULP finally enjoyed their first Number One with their seventh album, 'Different Class', which went straight into the chart at pole position in the first week of its release, in November 1995.

This was more than mere knee-jerk reacting on the part of the public, buying a record by a group who they now believed were so hip they just had to get into them – 'Different Class' was by far Pulp's best, most consistent LP to date.

Far more varied in terms of mood, tone and musical style than 'His 'N' Hers', these were also the strongest set of songs Pulp had ever written. 'Different Class' was the finest LP of the year, arguably better even than Blur's 'The Great Escape', Tricky's 'Maxinquaye', Supergrass' 'I Should Coco' and Black Grape's 'It's Great When You're Straight . . . Yeah!' If Pulp didn't win a Brit award for 'Common People', they would with this superlative long-player.

Apart from 'Mis-Shapes', 'Common People', 'Sorted For E's And Wizz' and 'Underwear', there was the dramatic tale of revenge set to Seventies TV theme music that was 'I Spy'; and the fantastic, superbly arranged and climactic 'Feelings Called Love', which was possibly Pulp's greatest track yet. 'Pencil Skirt', 'Live Bed Show', 'Disco 2000' (whose guitar riff is oddly reminiscent of Elton John's 'Saturday Night's Alright For Fighting'!), 'Monday Morning' and 'Bar Italia' were five more glorious

From cult obscurity to media icon in 18 years. Fast work, Jarvis!

examinations of Nineties Britain's sexual and social mores, Pulp-style.

'I suppose if you have a certain amount of success, you feel as though you've had a kind of kite-mark on you, do you know what I mean?' Jarvis said to me in 1995, self-deprecating to the end. 'Because I always used to feel like a marginal character, kind of stuck on the sidelines. And now I feel like, finally, I'm fit for human consumption.

'It's been a long, strange trip, all right, but I wouldn't have missed it for the world. In fact, I'd recommend anyone else out there to waste their life in the same manner as I have done, because it's been very, very enjoyable.'